The Business of Being Social

A practical guide to harnessing the power of Facebook, Twitter, LinkedIn and YouTube for all businesses

Michelle Carvill and
David Taylor

crimson

For my parents – *David Taylor*

The Business of Being Social

This edition first published in Great Britain in 2013 by Crimson Publishing Ltd, Westminster House, Kew Road, Richmond, Surrey TW9 2ND

© Michelle Carvill and David Taylor, 2013

The right of Michelle Carvill and David Taylor to be identified as the authors of this work has been asserted by them in accordance with the Copyright, Designs and Patents Act 1988.

British Library Cataloguing in Publication Data
A catalogue record for this book is available from the British Library.

ISBN 978 1 78059 170 4

Typeset by IDSUK (DataConnection) Ltd
Printed and bound in the UK by Bell & Bain Ltd, Glasgow

Publisher's note

Every possible effort has been made to ensure that the information contained in this book is accurate at the time of going to press, and the publishers and authors cannot accept responsibility for any errors or omissions, however caused. LinkedIn, Facebook, Twitter and YouTube have kindly granted permission for the use of their logos on the cover, but these organisations would like to clearly state that use of such logos does not constitute an endorsement of the book or its contents.

The Business of Being Social

Contents

Contents

Introduction

Over the past two years, as trainers for Business Training Made Simple, we have helped well over 1,500 professionals from a wide range of industries, both here in the UK and overseas, understand how they can get the most out of social media.

During this time, we have also observed how the social networks have morphed from simple devices used by individuals for pleasure into highly sophisticated marketing and communication tools.

This means that people have all sorts of preconceptions about what social media is, what it can and cannot do, what it can be used for, how they can measure its effectiveness, and what the **big** thing is.

In our courses, we've seen three groups of delegates who reflect this:

1. The complete sceptics who believe that social networks are simply a waste of effort. (Usually they've been pushed to attend a social media training course by a senior executive.) Or it may be that they've had their fingers burned by leaping on the social bandwagon without fully appreciating the necessity to take a strategic approach.
2. The curious ones who know that social media is heralding a seismic change in the way that we communicate but don't understand how to leverage this in their own organisations and are also apprehensive about the implications of opening the doors to becoming a 'conversational' organisation.
3. The early adopters on social networks who are keen to leverage the potentially far-reaching and powerful social media channels.

This book is aimed at all three audiences.

We start with basic business, marketing and communications principles, move on to strategy and planning, and then explore in detail the key social media sites.

Taking this approach means that *The Business of Being Social* will be of value to a wide range of people because it covers the many different subject areas affected by social networks, including sales, marketing, human resources, recruitment, media and public relations, customer relations and internal communications.

So whether you simply want to understand how to get the most use out of leveraging hashtags (#), want to explore how to use Facebook pay-per-click advertising or need ideas about creating a social media culture in your organisation, you will find plenty of practical tips and tactics within this book.

At the same time, we aim to debunk the five key myths about social media marketing – or 'social' for short.

1. **It is free.** The platforms are, but managing them and feeding them is certainly not.
2. **You have to do it all.** You don't, just as with any other form of marketing or communications.
3. **It's only for kids.** Thirty-, forty-, fifty-, sixty- and seventy-somethings are adapting to social in much the same way they did to email, the internet and Google.
4. **Set up accounts and magic will happen.** You wish! The evidence from the huge number of companies who start, then give up when it doesn't deliver instant results, says that this simply isn't the case.
5. **You can share absolutely anything.** We live in an age where content is still king, particularly on social. Therefore it's got to be good! After all, you are what you share and your brand and company reputation is at stake.

As with our training courses, at the end of every chapter in this book we include a Social Media Marketing Action Plan with some simple tips on what you should think about doing. We also include a glossary at the end of the book with explanations of many of the most commonly used terms in social media.

For many readers, this should be seen as the start of the journey into making the best possible use of social media. The trick now is to keep learning, to put into practice the information in this book and, most importantly, to stay abreast of new developments. (Because, believe us, the platforms are constantly changing.)

We've created a blog to run alongside the book (www.thebusinessof beingsocial.co.uk), as well as a Twitter account (@BOBSthebook). That way we can keep you informed about what is happening in social media, and we can make sure that you can get information that's bang up to date – important in a world where a week can be a long time!

Enjoy the book, and be sure to share your feedback and questions with us. After all – this book is the start of many a conversation.

Best wishes
Michelle Carvill and David Taylor

1 | Welcome to the social media age

What you will learn from this chapter:

- Background to the social networks
- How social media has become part of our daily lives
- Statistics showing that social media is a truly global phenomenon
- Importance of using social media to deliver on your business objectives
- How to integrate social media into your overall marketing plans
- Blending traditional and social media
- Instigating continuous conversations rather than start-stop campaigns

History can be seen as a series of events that, taken together, make the world what it is today. Technological innovation has played a major role in history, from the invention of the telephone in 1876, radio in 1896, television in 1925, the first computer in 1926 and the World Wide Web in 1990.

Here are four more dates that we could add to this list:

- 5 May 2003 – LinkedIn
- 4 February 2004 – Facebook
- 23 April 2005 – YouTube
- 21 March 2006 – Twitter.

None of these networks is more than 10 years old but, together with the development of smartphones in 2000 and the introduction of 3G internet in 2002, these platforms have totally transformed the way in which we communicate and, indeed, do business.

In the space of just one decade, these four key social networks, plus a vast number of smaller ones, have achieved a level of global reach that other media could only dream about.

At the time of writing, Facebook now has over 1 billion members, Twitter over 500 million, LinkedIn 187 million, YouTube over 800 million and Google+ 400 million. These are staggering figures and they illustrate the enormous penetration that these sites have had in a comparatively short space of time.

A report by www.emarketer.com in March 2012 estimated that by the end of that year there would be 1.43 billion social network users, a 19.2% increase over 2011. It also predicted that '63.2% of internet users will visit a social network at least once a month, rising to 67.6% in 2013 and 70.7% in 2014. At those user rates, one out of every five people in the world will use a social network this year, and one in every four will do so in 2014.' (Read more at www.emarketer.com/Article.aspx?R=ten08903).

Let's break these statistics down into the five current key social networks: Facebook, Twitter, LinkedIn, YouTube and Google+.

Facebook

Set up as a way for friends to communicate easily with each other online and with the mission statement, 'to give people the power to share and make the world more open and connected', Facebook has grown into a media giant.

Floated on the Nasdaq in May 2012, the company has its eye on taking on the internet itself by offering users an alternative to the World Wide Web. And with the introduction of Timeline brand pages, Facebook is geared to pose a credible threat to consumer-facing websites.

Facebook was initially hampered by the fact that it wasn't originally designed to be viewed on mobile devices. With increasing pressure from investors to deliver a return on their investment following the initial public offering (IPO), the site had to find a way of turning a profit from advertising on mobile platforms. During the course of 2012, Facebook worked hard to make its site as easy to use on an Apple or Android device as a PC, as well as introducing a new range of advertising products.

Statistics from www.internetworldstats.com illustrate how the site has achieved such a premier position within social networking. Their figures show the numbers of accounts per region:

- Europe 232.8m
- Asia 195m
- North America 173.2m
- South America 112.5m
- Africa 41.3m
- Middle East 20.2m
- Oceania/Australia 13.6m
- The Caribbean 6.3m.

Looking more closely into the demographics of Facebook, a study by www.onlinemba.com came up with the following results:

- 57% of users were female
- 46% of users were aged 45 and over
- users aged 34 and under made up only 32% of the total
- 81% of users were educated to college or degree level
- 56% had an income of $50,000 or more.

Looking at Facebook use on mobile devices, research by www.socialbakers.com in August 2012 found that the site had 488 million mobile users: in other words, roughly half of those accessing Facebook globally were doing so from their phones or tablet devices.

In addition, the study showed that the reach is even bigger in countries such as South Africa, Nigeria and Japan, where 70– 80% of users access the site from mobile devices. (See the full report here: www.socialbakers.com/blog/554-facebook-hits-488-million-mobile-users-infographic.)

Twitter

Originally set up as a more advanced way of texting, Twitter limits users to just 140 characters in which to tell people what they are doing. The site's mission statement is 'To instantly connect people everywhere to what's most important to them.'

Since its launch, Twitter has morphed into one of the most sophisticated marketing and communication tools that has ever existed. With hundreds of applications designed around accessing Twitter via PCs and mobile devices, this social network is now an important part of many organisations' marketing and communication strategies.

Data from www.webanalyticsworld.net shows the top five countries in terms of Twitter accounts:

1. USA 107.7m
2. Brazil 33.3m
3. Japan 29.9m
4. UK 23.8m
5. Indonesia 19.5m.

These are the demographics for Twitter from the www.onlinemba.com study:

- 59% of users were female
- 58% of users were aged 35 and over
- users aged up to 24 made up 19% of the total
- 83% of users were educated to college or degree level
- 47% had an income of $50,000 or more.

In contrast to Facebook, according to Twitter's own statistics in June 2012, 60% of users globally accessed the site via mobile devices. In the UK, a study by the *Guardian* newspaper found that over 80% of users accessed Twitter via mobiles (http://econsultancy.com/uk/blog/9884-twitter-hits-tenm-uk-users-80-use-mobile). Interestingly, 40% of Twitter users have never tweeted – however, they depend on the platform as a key resource for up-to-date news.

LinkedIn

Originally set up as a recruitment resource, LinkedIn can now be classed as the Facebook of the business world. Its mission statement reads, 'Connecting the world's professionals to make them more productive and successful.'

LinkedIn is increasingly being used not only as a brand-building device for individuals but also as the first port of call for researchers looking for information about companies. For many business to business (B2B) firms, and increasingly for consumer-facing organisations, their LinkedIn Company profile can often be as important as their website because it contains information about their most valuable commodity – their staff.

According to LinkedIn's own data (www.slideshare.net/amover/linkedin-demographics-statistics-jan-2012) the top five countries in terms of members are:

1. USA 58.5m
2. India 13.3m
3. UK 8.4m
4. Brazil 6.8m
5. Canada 5.1m.

Data from the www.onlinemba.com study reveals these statistics about the site:

- there was a 50/50 split of male/female users
- 81% of users were aged 35 and over
- those users aged up to 24 made up 19% of the total
- 87% of users were educated to college or degree level
- 72% had an income of $50,000 or more
- there were two million companies on the site.

Other information from LinkedIn about its members:

- 44% of users work in companies with 10,000 or more employees
- 39% of members are managers, directors, chief officers or vice presidents
- the countries with the strongest growth in members were Indonesia, Turkey and Brazil

- the industries with the highest concentration worldwide were high-tech (14.3%), finance (12.4%) and manufacturing (10.1%).

YouTube

Originally set up as a video sharing site, YouTube is now the third most visited website and the second most used search engine in the world.

According to YouTube's own statistics (www.youtube.com/t/press_statistics) the site has over 800 million users each month. Other useful information includes the following:

- 70% of YouTube traffic comes from outside the USA
- YouTube is localised in 43 countries and across 60 languages
- traffic from mobile devices trebled in 2011
- more than 20% of global YouTube views come from mobile devices
- three hours of video is uploaded per minute to YouTube from mobile devices
- YouTube is available on 350 million devices.

Google+

Launched in June 2011 (much later than the other social networks), Google+ now has around 400 million users and is fully integrated with the full suite of Google offerings, including YouTube.

Built around the traditional social networking platform of a central news feed, what differentiates Google+ is the option to segment your network of contacts into Circles. In addition, in the context of an overall search engine optimisation strategy, content posted on Google+ has been shown to assist an organisation's ranking on Google.

According to the www.onlinemba.com study, 71% of users are male, and almost 44% of users were classed as being single.

How social and mobile media have changed the way we communicate

People and organisations have always had to rely on third parties to be able to communicate with mass audiences.

Advertising in flyers, pamphlets, newspapers, magazines, radio and TV, or undertaking public relations campaigns, were the only realistic ways to get visibility for your brand.

The ability to get your voice heard changed with the advent of the internet, and more recently has become even easier via smartphones and mobile-enabled social networks. Very simply, there has been a complete democratisation in the way we communicate. With just a phone and internet access, anyone in the world can be a publisher, broadcaster or editor.

This shift is extremely powerful and has deep ramifications not just for marketing but also for sales, human resources, recruitment, public relations, brand protection, customer services and internal communications. It even has an impact on how organisations are structured.

Giving staff, clients, customers and stakeholders a voice can offer up a range of opportunities as well as major challenges for organisations. As a result, we are moving into the age of the social business, in which all aspects of an organisation are influenced by social media.

According to Gartner, Inc. (www.gartner.com/it/page.jsp?id=1278413), by the end of 2013 more people will use mobile devices than computers to go online, heralding the start of the true mobile internet age. Now millions of people aren't just *on* social networks, they are *in* them. The truly connected consumer has moved away from 'linear conversations'.

Most businesses, at some point in their life, will have professed to want to *truly understand* customer needs. For decades marketers and customer service departments have run customer surveys or focus groups in an attempt to get closer to their customers and to enable them to fully understand their customers' needs.

Why? In a nutshell, because as markets have become more and more crowded, customer service has become an important differentiator, and the service delivery 'bar' has been well and truly raised, along with customer expectation. It's now commonplace for organisations' strategic plans to include the aim of being seen to be 'listening to the customer'.

Over the years, the mechanisms for researching and delivering customer needs have been vast and varied, and many organisations have created whole new departments to deal with the important subject.

Technology has enabled the systemisation of data and information capture, so that, as customers, we're continuously and seamlessly able to share our *views and needs* with the organisation. We can have a continuous conversation with the people we're buying products and services from. But it's not always a seamless process.

Now, through social networking platforms, not only are we able to share our views directly with the organisation, but at the same time we're also able to share our views with anyone else who is willing to listen too – our friends, family, strangers, other prospective purchasers – whoever.

'Social media' are exactly what the phrase implies:

- **Media:** content of some form. It could be promotional or advisory; it could be a blog about a new product release, or a story about a dreadful customer experience. It can be delivered in a range of formats – the written word, video, still images, etc.

- **Social:** rather than a linear, one-way conversation (e.g. a brand broadcasting a message to its audience) it's a shared or *networked conversation*. Others can share it, pass it on, comment and consume.

What this means for businesses is that a great or dreadful customer experience, product or promotion can be shared. It can go viral and reach untold numbers of people at the touch of a button.

A continuous conversation

The floodgates to conversation marketing are well and truly open . . . and that conversation is 'continuous'.

One-to-one, one-to-many, many-to-many conversations

We have moved away from a traditional 'linear' conversation, in which the brand or organisation would promote their message or offering and people could merely consume it if they liked it, or not consume it if they didn't; and perhaps they might talk offline about it.

Instead we now have a truly 'networked' conversation where people can not only talk with their peers, friends and strangers, but also have direct conversations with the brands and businesses too.

Businesses that pay lip service to wanting to understand customer needs can no longer hide behind the annual customer survey. Consumers are beginning to expect to have a direct dialogue with a brand, product or service.

For many large monolithic organisations that are embroiled in red tape and make policies and decisions by committee, getting to grips with such an open dialogue is terrifying.

To be a social business means implementing genuine and transparent channels of communication. It's about opening the doors to listen to what customers have to say and, where necessary, creating a new set of policies for safeguarding and managing 'social media marketing' responsibility.

There's no getting away from 'listening to what customers really want' because there are conversations happening all the time – conversations that businesses can choose to ignore (at their peril) or embrace.

We're now living in an 'always on' society

Given the pace at which social media are being embraced by all sectors of society, and the ever-growing pace of technology, businesses that don't 'get' social media are seriously likely to get left behind.

We love the statement regularly shared by strategist and author (and probably one of the people talking the most sense about social media strategy), Brian Solis (@briansolis): 'We are in the age of digital Darwinism – organisations need to adapt or die.'

If your business isn't part of the conversation, you might ask yourself, in the words of the Socialnomics team, 'The ROI [return on investment] of social media is, will your business still be around in five years?'

Think before you dive in

If we view social media platforms as far-reaching communication channels, that poses the question of *how* organisations can leverage these channels to deliver on business objectives.

The remit of any marketing strategy is to deliver on the business objectives – ultimately driving activity to achieve results that make sense for the business. Social media isn't something an organisation does just for the sake of doing social media (because everyone else is!) but, rather, something you do to deliver on specific business objectives, as part of a well-defined marketing strategy.

Business owners, CEOs and marketing directors should be thinking *how* they can plug social media into what they currently do to leverage what the platforms offer (and, remember, each platform offers some-thing different) and ultimately deliver on their objectives.

However, probably as a result of eagerness to get onto the channels, businesses often dive into social media without any real thinking or planning. This simple model (adapted from the brilliant book by Olivier Blanchard, *Social Media ROI*) outlines in a very simple way a strategic approach to social media.

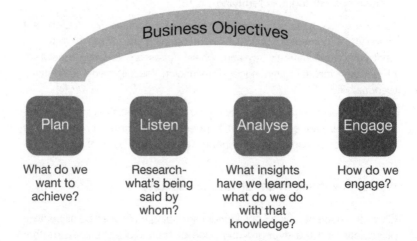

As marketing and communication strategists, we have spent a significant number of years developing communication and marketing strategies for clients. To date, we're both unaware of any other marketing or communication activity where a business would just dive in without any thinking, planning or research.

Far too often, both in our training and in our consulting lives, when we ask business people the question, 'So, you're on Twitter – what's the objective of the channel?', we're met with blank faces, or answers such as, 'Well, we saw that our competitors were on Twitter so we thought we'd better get on it too.'

In our view, these far-reaching communication channels require even more planning and thinking than usual, and that's because they are resource-hungry channels.

Hungry channels need regular feeding

There are few things more pointless than approaching a Twitter channel thinking, 'I'm not sure what we should be tweeting about.' This is where taking a strategic approach comes in. With any other strategic project, you would always embark on some research to learn about your audiences. The same goes for social audiences.

Understanding your business objectives and how each channel works is absolutely key – and there are seven (if not more) reasons why.

1.   If you have clear objectives, you know what you are listening for.
2.   You know who you are looking to target.
3.   You can research effectively – which channels are your target audience using?
4.   You can understand who is influential and who you need to be befriending.
5.   You know who to listen to and what they are saying (and you should listen more than you talk – more on that later).
6.   Having listened, you will have gained useful insights into consumer needs.
7.   You're better able to direct and create useful content/conversations.

As Michael Gerber says in his book *The E-Myth*:

> *Those that aim for nothing, hit it with remarkable accuracy.*

So you need to be sure that you have set specific objectives and that you have a very clear understanding of the purpose of your social media activity (and indeed any other activity).

It is easy to understand why businesses dive in and start engaging. The channels have deliberately been made very user friendly and therefore setting up accounts is simple. No expert or coding knowledge is required; all you need to do is fill out a few simple fields and you're away.

And, of course, all the social platforms are currently free (though this may change down the line). You can set up a Facebook Page, a Google+ page, a Twitter, LinkedIn or YouTube account for absolutely no cost. Anyone can do it. And so they do.

However, the key is to ensure that you are (as the sub-title of this book describes) *harnessing the power* of these channels – optimising them to deliver on your specific objectives.

As any good craftsperson will tell you, you can make your life simpler if you use the right tools for the job. However, it is what you do with the tools that matters. Remember, anyone can use the tools, anyone can engage with them, so standing out from the crowd and ensuring you're using them effectively is absolutely vital. The channels are merely the platforms that enable mass communication. What you do with them is the all-important element.

When getting started, a basic plan is better than no plan. So, following the simple four step framework – Plan, Listen, Analyse, Engage – will at least enable you to follow a process of thinking, listening and learning – before you engage.

Blending social media into your marketing mix

Social media don't just impact on the promotional side of your business. Day to day they are leveraged in customer services, HR (human resources) and other key areas of your business. However, the uptake for these new, far-reaching communication channels does seem to have been dominated by marketing. A common objective of delegates on our training courses is, 'We want to learn how to integrate social media into our marketing activities.'

Traditional and social: a complementary model

As we have discussed, social media marketing is gathering momentum, but traditional marketing channels still very much have their place. Rather than seeing the two as different disciplines, you should view them as complementary to one another.

For example, television is a traditional vehicle, and methods of engaging and interacting with viewers of a television programme might involve an invitation to 'Call us on 0800 . . .' or 'Email us on . . .'. Now it's commonplace for television programmes (think Sky News, for example) to invite their audience to tweet them pictures or questions. Some of the rawest footage is filmed not by stealthy cameramen, but by Joe or Jane

Public, who just happened to get a dramatic or newsworthy picture on their iPhone.

Similarly, hashtags (#) are promoted both at the beginning of and during programmes. The hashtag (which we'll discuss in more detail later) enables people to engage with a potentially global audience all talking about what's happening on the programme.

During the recent Channel 4 programme *Bank of Dave*, the hashtag #bankofdave was promoted approximately 12 times. Each time the hashtag aired, activity around it on Twitter was buzzing. This is a perfect example of a traditional channel blending social media to leverage activity and further amplify the message.

Glee, the hit TV show, is one of the most tweeted-about programmes. That's largely because as it airs, its actors, the stars of the show, also go on to Twitter and engage with their fans. This takes engaging the user to a whole new dimension. The user has to watch the programme *when it airs* (not later via on-demand TV such as iPlayer and TiVo) so that they can join the real-time conversation on Twitter. Remember, the programme isn't live, but the tweeting is.

So whatever your activity is – television show, trade press advertise-ment, station billboard, direct mail piece, email, newsletter or door drop – consider how you can plug in to social media to keep the conver-sation going.

Here's another business to business (B2B) example.

An event was held in Glasgow last year by the networking organisa-tion Business Networking International (BNI). Their 2012 European Conference had its own hashtag, #BNIEC, and, as you would expect from an organisation of networkers, it served as a way for people to network online as well as offline.

Acting as a virtual conversation, #BNIEC enabled people, both at the conference and in the wider world, to network before, during and after the event.

It was even possible to measure the effectiveness of the hashtag using a tool such as Tweetreach (www.tweetreach.com) (see Chapter 4).

Planning

Start with the end in mind

Our advice for people who are undertaking strategic planning is to start with the end in mind. When you know what you want to achieve, you can plan effectively.

From a practical perspective, typical questions you could ask at the planning stage include:

- What are our objectives? (The *why*.)
- What is the key message?
- Who are the target audience?
- What is market research telling us?
- What's our USP? (Unique selling proposition.)
- What are our competitors doing?
- What are our tactics? (The *what*.)
- Which channels are we going to use? (Direct mail, billboard, PR etc.)
- Where shall we send people? (Website, call centre, landing page.)
- How do we incentivise them?
- Are we resourced effectively?
- What's our tone of voice?
- What are we going to share?
- What's our compelling content?
- What are our keywords? (More on the importance of these later.)

Planning template

Our advice at the planning stage is that when you get to the 'tactical' element of what you are actually going to do, you need to be thinking, 'How do we plug social media channels into these activities?'

And, of course, the social channels broaden the scope of your planning. We can look at some of the typical traditional questions in another way.

1 What is the goal?

This remains the dominant feature of planning. The goal (as mentioned before) is the *business goal* rather than the communications goal.

2 Who is the audience?

You can get really very 'human' in your exploration here. Go beyond the typical demographics that focus on age and location, and instead ask yourself: 'What does our audience look like? What's their frame of mind right now? Who are they influenced by?'

3 Where is the audience?

Which social channels are they using? Mostly one particular channel, or many different ones? Where are they based – UK or overseas? Therefore, what time does your social activity need to be scheduled for?

4 How do we connect in a compelling way?

This isn't just about getting people to Like your Facebook Page. It's more about thinking creatively about what you know about the audience and what is going to engage them – and, hopefully, compel them to share and get others engaged.

5 How do we keep the conversation continuous?

It's not just about getting that Twitter follower or running a promotion to get people to Like your page. As we'll see in the Facebook chapter, the Like is the equivalent of getting someone to walk through the door. Getting them to linger, buy, and become advocates of what you do is another thing. So you need to be thinking about a longer-term engagement.

6 How do we get our audience to recommend us to others?

I'm sure you'll agree that 'word of mouth' is a powerful source of new business generation. With social media, the virality potential of the channels and the ease with which one person can share content with another (and another, and another . . .), thereby quickly amplifying the message, is something that should be thoroughly considered. It isn't even identified in many marketing plans we've seen!

Putting in the right effort at the start pays off

Most projects or initiatives tend to be front-loaded, and social media activity is no different. The analogy we make in our social media training or consulting sessions is that of a plane taking off.

The more thinking and planning you do with your social media platforms, the more effective they will become.

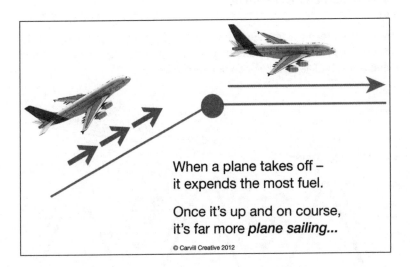

When a plane takes off –
it expends the most fuel.

Once it's up and on course,
it's far more *plane sailing...*

© Carvill Creative 2012

Taking a targeted approach

If you take some time to research who are the key influencers in your space and make the effort to target them, connect with them and nurture them so that they become key advocates, that's likely to be far more productive than what we refer to as 'machine gun social media' – following anyone and everyone in the hope that someone will be right.

Building a network of influencers and an audience that is targeted to deliver on your business objectives will get you to the circle on the aeroplane diagram – and that's what we refer to as the 'sweet point' of your activity.

At that point, your social activity tends to create a life of its own. Of course you will have to remain focused on your objectives, but the nature of what you are creating and the engagement level of those you engage with will have created some advocates. Those advocates then start to share on your behalf and bring others to you. Effort becomes shared.

The way you get to that sweet point will be different for each platform and each business. Down the line someone will develop a formula that relates methodology and time to outcome. But for now, when these channels are still very fertile territory, we can't share with you any magic timescales or numbers – just a robust methodology that we've been utilising with our clients over the past few years.

Continuous conversations versus stop-start marketing

Many marketing campaigns have a kind of stop-start element to them. Think about your marketing plans or activity plans and you'll see that the schedule usually goes something like this.

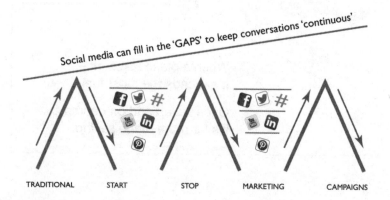

To demonstrate the point, let's say we're marketing an annual conference for all the members who read this book and sign up to the blog. The event – the Business of Being Social, or BOBS for short – is scheduled for September 2014 and all BOBS readers will be invited to attend. The planning will start months in advance, some teaser activity will take place a good few months before, and there will be a strong push of marketing activity approximately six to eight weeks before the event itself.

Let's take a look at how this could play out.

BOBS conference planning

Event date: 17 September 2014.

Some teaser introductory activity before the hard marketing push:

- **December 2013:** 'save the date' message included in Christmas cards sent to all members.
- **April, May, June:** members' newsletter includes a reminder of the Annual Conference and showcases where, when, what, who, etc.
- **1 June:** campaign starts in earnest. Three rounds of emails, sent two weeks apart, encourage users to book online and include various early bird promotions. This activity runs to mid-July.
- **Late July:** telesales activity commences, sweeping up those members who have been invited, haven't declined and haven't booked. This activity runs through to mid-August.
- **Mid- to late August:** last push campaign. Email and telesales to encourage as many members as possible to come to the event.

This activity demonstrates the 'stop-start' nature of marketing activity. Messages were sent out in December, April and May, and then some in June. Each time you 'push' out an activity, you are almost starting again from scratch.

People who read the 'save the date' cards in December but didn't respond will have forgotten all about the communication and will be reminded when you spring it on them in April. Those that receive the May email reminder may or may not remember the promotion in April. The hope is that the more you push a continuous message, the more 'share of mind' you are building. But there are gaps in the middle. As consumers, we are bombarded by messages all the time. Research shows that we don't remember all of them.

Continuous conversations

Now let's look at some ideas about how you can leverage your communications by including social media to make a conversation continuous.

Making the conversation continuous

- Let's say that in the December communication you showcase a hashtag for the event – #annualconfBOBS (there's more on demystifying hashtags in Chapter 4).
- You encourage all your members who are already on Twitter to follow the hashtag for updates and special insights – perhaps even incentivising engagement via competitions and offers.
- Further, to build awareness of the event and BOBS, you encourage your members to share the hashtag and you use the hashtag to promote the great content you're providing.
- Over on Facebook, you get each of the conference participants to come online to answer marketing, digital or social media questions. You promote these 'live chats' both on Twitter and in your newsletters to encourage as much traction as possible.
- The hashtag for the event is included on all marketing promotional materials, in your newsletters, on your email footers, on any press ads, etc., so that you continuously encourage people to join the conversation.
- If people advise that they can't make the event you can still encourage them to join the event 'virtually' by simply tuning into the event on the day via the #annualconfBOBS hashtag.
- After the event the hashtag lives on. People can still converse and share. Ideally, you should track all uses of the hashtag and save all those people who joined that hashtag conversation into a Twitter list (more on Twitter Lists in Chapter 4).
- Make sure that you 'followed' them and encouraged them to come and ask questions on your Facebook Page.
- Watch the conversations around the hashtag and the questions raised to provide you with a steer for creating new and relevant content.
- Address any positive or negative elements – listening to what people say will give you useful insights into what you could do better next time.
- Endeavour to continue the conversation. Having engaged people in relation to the event in the first year, try to keep that conversation going so that by year two you will have built some advocates.
- Continue to create content that is useful and purposeful, encourage people to download it from your website and capture their email addresses. This helps build your database in a targeted and purposeful way.

This simple example demonstrates the difference between a stilted, stop-start approach and one in which blending traditional and social media creates a more joined-up and continuous approach.

Traditional and social media are truly complementary. Indeed, where traditional is becoming more challenging, getting creative and blending in social elements can be a powerful tactic when applied effectively. The thinking and planning still has to be very 'joined up'.

Social media marketing action plan

- Plan effectively.
- Establish the purpose of each marketing channel.
- Decide on your tone of voice.
- Reflect the correct image for your brand.
- Take a targeted approach.
- Think about content. You are what you share – is what you're sharing doing you justice?
- Traditional versus social. A complementary model makes sense.

2| The many uses of social media

> What you will learn from this chapter:
> - Why it is important to have objectives for social media
> - How flexible social media can be
> - The different ways to use social media for business
> - Understanding how to apply these to your organisation

As we've mentioned, many organisations dive into social media without any real thinking or planning. Time and time again in our training courses, we come across people who have been told to attend by their boss or manager so that they can 'do' Twitter or 'do' Facebook, without really understanding why.

Similarly, over the past two or three years, thousands of organisations have jumped on the social media bandwagon either because their competitors have or because they've felt pressured into doing it to keep abreast of the times. They often have very little understanding about why they should be embarking on a social media strategy, which channels they should be employing or, indeed, how it will benefit them as an organisation.

We have set out the importance of having a targeted approach and meeting specific business objectives using social media. Now we need to look at the ways in which social media can be used to achieve these targets.

Unfortunately, people make assumptions about social media. It is often seen as a cure-all to solve all marketing problems or a quick fix to increase customer engagement. It can even be used as yet another 'outbound' or broadcast marketing tool to spam potential customers.

Clearly, like any other form of technology, social media can be used in a variety of different ways – for good or ill – and there will often be occasions when organisations use the same social networks for entirely different purposes.

But it is vital for any brand to have a properly delineated strategy for using social media so that it doesn't waste time or money just doing it for the sake of doing it. Without this in place, the results will be disappointing and could even be harmful.

In this chapter, we identify a number of key ways that organisations can use social networks to meet specific objectives. These vary from customer service to lead generation and from news distribution to product promotion. There are also case studies of how platforms have been successfully employed.

What will become evident is the fact that social media impacts not only on marketing but on many other areas of business including sales, customer service, media relations, HR and CSR (corporate and social responsibility).

Customer support and service

In the past, if a customer had an issue about a product or service, they would have had to write in or speak to a complaints department. In recent years, customers with queries or complaints have been diverted to a call centre in another country, often further infuriating them and providing inadequate levels of customer support.

With the advent of social networks, customers can now bypass these traditional channels and communicate directly with brands via sites like Facebook or Twitter. This can be done in two different ways, each of which requires a different approach. People either access a brand's online social media presence and start a conversation or they use their own social media profiles to voice their concerns or complaints.

Brands like Vodafone (www.facebook.com/vodafoneuk) and Delta Airlines (@deltaAssist) use social channels as specific customer service tools. Individual, and in many cases named, customer support staff answer queries online, and most of these queries remain in the public domain.

However, it is also possible to have private conversations on both Facebook and Twitter. On Twitter you need to get the person to follow you before you can send them a direct (i.e. private) message. On Facebook, you need to go to your Page's admin settings and tick the box that says 'Show Message Button'. This enables any Facebook user – whether or not they Like your Page – to send the Page a direct (private) message. You can then respond to this message. (Note: you cannot initiate private conversations with people from your Facebook Page – more on this in Chapter 5.)

Clearly, if your objective is to use social media as a customer support channel, you need to ensure that you have the policies and procedures in place to do it properly. These may include:

- round-the-clock monitoring of your site(s)
- dedicated and correctly trained staff to deal with complaints

- close collaboration between internal departments to ensure a joined-up approach.

A recent study in the USA by STELLAService shows which brands are using social media most effectively for customer service. You can find out more at http://moneyland.time.com/2012/06/01/customer-service-via-twitter-some-companies-are-on-it-others-not-so-much.

What's clear is that Twitter, and no doubt Facebook, are being closely watched by the large corporations. Brand reputation is clearly being managed very closely online, with the remit to capture any negativity before it spirals out of control and does real damage.

Let's hope that more and more businesses start to use Twitter not only as a means of responding to customer queries but also as a way to add real value. Most customers would much rather deal with a ten-minute response than a 90-minute one. That would speak volumes for a brand – the fact that they are actually giving a service to their customers, rather than simply aiming to preserve their brand reputation. The two are interlinked.

Being responsive in the social media arena can't just be about apologies – it's got to be about servicing the consumer. So take heed, any organisations who are simply jumping on the Twitter bandwagon. Don't just pay lip service and make your presence all about managing your brand reputation. Get a proper customer support service running via Twitter and really make your presence count!

Brand reputation management

While it is important that you manage your own online presence, it is also vital that you monitor what is being said about you elsewhere online, whether in blogs, forums or social media sites.

Just as media relations is about protecting your brand in the public domain, so social media relations is about ensuring that you are on top of what is being said about you online – and dealing with it in a professional and well-thought-through manner. The consequences of remaining completely in the dark could be pretty serious.

Monitoring what is being said – both positive and negative – online about your brand can be done in a number of ways which we will touch on here but expand further in Chapter 8.

Regularly putting your organisation's name into the search bars of the key social networking sites or setting up alerts – simple ones via Google Alert (www.google.com/alerts) and tools like www.socialmention.com – enables you to stay on top of any issues and react swiftly if you need to. (More tools are discussed in Chapter 8.)

Speed of response is the key. Traditionally, when a negative story broke in the press, organisations would be forewarned and would be able to prepare some form of response or rebuttal. Experienced press officers will know all about this. For large customer-facing organisations with a high-profile media presence, 'lines to take' have to be prepared, as do crisis communication strategies. In addition, press officers need to be on an on-call rota to ensure 24-hour media relations cover.

In the social media age, when people can post on Facebook walls or on Twitter 24 hours a day, the same discipline needs to be applied, but you have far less time to defend your brand. As a result, community managers working for organisations that serve the public out of normal office hours – restaurants, bars, clubs, transport companies, etc. – need to monitor sites 24/7 to ensure that damaging comments are dealt with and queries are not left unanswered.

Social story

This real-life story is a great example of how some top-end brands aren't monitoring what is being said about them online.

One of our friends bought a coat from a luxury retailer for £300, and was assured that she could return the coat within 14 days of purchase. When she got it home she discovered that her boyfriend had bought the exact same coat for her for Christmas. Touched by this unusual display of attentiveness from her partner, she took one of the coats back to the shop in order to get a refund.

Unfortunately, they explained, they didn't offer refunds unless the item was faulty and she was only entitled to a £300 gift voucher or exchange! (Apparently the small print on the receipt explained this.) Tearful and distressed, she had no choice but to leave the shop with the coat, in the hope that the retailer's higher powers would view this situation as very unfortunate and see it as an opportunity to offer a high standard of customer service out of good will.

They did completely the opposite. Not only did they refuse any form of refund, two emails she sent to two separate people were completely ignored. Being ignored not only annoyed her but also encouraged her to take further action – she decided to use social media to get her voice heard. She wrote a blog post about her experience, and naturally shared it via Twitter. She also searched for the brand in the hope that they too were on Twitter and that she could share the blog post with them and get some customer service joy via the channel.

When she did her search for the brand, she discovered not only that they didn't appear to have any formal presence on Twitter but also that many others in a similar situation to her were also talking about the brand, and about their grievances with the 'no refunds' policy.

She also found that tweeters were sharing tried and tested tips and tactics for how to damage the garments – because if the product was deemed faulty, a full refund was permissible.

At this point she decided to inform the brand of both her blog post and indeed all the comments she had found on Twitter. They had not been listening. They did not know this was going on.

Eventually the company did offer her a full refund and apologised for not responding promptly to her emails. They also thanked her for sharing what she had found on Twitter and promised to act on the negative comments. But how much damage had already been done to their brand, let alone their garments?

Interestingly, this brand is now firmly on Twitter, but not, in our view, doing a great job of it. They've taken to the channel in the only way they know how – 'broadcast media' – and are pushing traditional-style messaging into a conversational channel. (More on this in Chapter 3.)

Polling and product feedback

One of the key aspects of social media is the art of listening and promoting high levels of engagement, which we will come to in Chapter 8.

At the same time, because we are in such a rapidly evolving marketplace where customers' buying choices are determined by so many different factors, it is useful to gauge what people think about not only your products and services but also a wide range of other subjects.

Finally, the more feedback you get on your posts and comments, the more visible you will be online. This is because all the social networks – as well as Google and even Amazon – encourage interaction and comments. The more engagement you get, the better placed you will be in both search engines and social media searches.

The likes of Facebook and LinkedIn know this, so both have some form of polling function built directly into their sites. Facebook allows polls to be conducted from personal profiles in the Update Status box and from the Event/Milestone drop-down menu on Pages. LinkedIn has its own polling feature, which can be accessed from a drop-down menu underneath the More tab.

Google+ and YouTube, in line with WordPress and most other social networking sites, allow people to comment on posts, updates and videos.

Meanwhile free apps such as Survey Monkey (www.surveymonkey.com) or Pollpigeon (www.pollpigeon.com) allow people to run their own polls or surveys.

One key advantage with polls is that they give people simple choices to make, thus making it more likely that you will get interaction. For example, Starbucks did a poll in August 2012, which asked fans to comment on when they thought ice cream was best.

A total of 31,900 people voted, but there would have been far fewer (if more varied) responses if Starbucks had left off polling options.

Polls can be pretty comprehensive and if done regularly can help brands to form a better understanding about the needs and thoughts of their customer base.

Lead generation

Many organisations incorrectly see social media as purely a lead generation tool. While there are many ways in which it is possible to drive sales leads – using both organic and paid-for methods – very often, social may not be as effective as, say, using pay-per-click on Google, email or even a PR campaign.

Much will rest on the nature of your organisation, your target audience and how you use the social channels to engage with audiences.

According to Hubspot (http://bit.ly/P8dCVJ), LinkedIn is the most successful social network for lead generation. The company found that traffic from this site 'generated the highest visitor-to-lead conversion rate at 2.74%, almost 3 times higher (277%) than both Twitter (.69%) and Facebook (.77%)'.

One of the key things to bear in mind when using social networks for lead generation is that on social media, you rarely sell directly. This would be seen as spamming and is likely to alienate your fans or followers. Instead, you create the conditions under which people will naturally want to do business with you. Remember, these are social networks. Networking takes time and effort. You need to get people to know you, like you, trust you – and ultimately to do business with you.

To build this trust and awareness we come back to the need for engaging, targeted content as well as specific calls to action and decent landing or splash pages.

In order to respond to leads, you've also got to be 'listening' in rather than simply using the channels as 'broadcast' platforms. Far better to respond to a need than simply to push out irrelevant noise.

Paid-for advertising on social media

One of the most successful ways of using social platforms for direct lead generation is by using paid-for methods including pay-per-click advertising or sponsored tweets, videos (YouTube) or stories (Facebook). Not only can these be used to drive traffic to your social media sites, they can also be a viable way to drive traffic to your website or specific landing page.

Pay-per-click advertising on social media channels works in a similar way to ads on Google. Adverts are put together, a target demographic is chosen, the advertiser then chooses how much they want to pay for each click and also what budget they are going to allocate. Ads will then appear within users' news feeds or, in the case of YouTube, within videos or video searches. The advertiser pays only if someone actually clicks on their ad.

Another viable way in which social media can be used for lead generation is through competitions, specifically on Facebook. Using specially designed apps within Facebook Pages, and abiding by Facebook's strict guidelines (www.facebook.com/ad_guidelines.php), it is possible to run successful campaigns. (More on this in Chapter 5.)

Case study: Chewton Glen Hotel

Chewton Glen Hotel in Hampshire (www.chewtonglen.com) used Facebook pay-per-click in 2012 to launch their new tree houses. They created a competition featuring an overnight stay for four in a Treehouse Suite as a prize. Using an app selected from www.woobox.com, a customised tab was then added to their Facebook Page, www.facebook.com/chewtonglenhotel.

To ensure that the competition spread virally, entrants were encouraged to Like the hotel's Page, after which a request for the entrant's email information appeared. To spread news of the competition, an option to post the competition information on the entrant's Facebook wall automatically appeared, encouraging them to post a synopsis of the prize, plus a direct link to a customised competition tab.

And to encourage sharing the competition virally, a further prompter confirming the competition entry carried another message to spread the good word.

The result was an increase in the Likes of their Page from 1,200 to 13,500. Over 2,000 Facebook users shared the competition on their own walls, which meant it was seen by close to 400,000 users. The hotel also saw increased activity on their website as well as receiving higher call volumes in all areas of operations.

News distribution and public relations

The PR profession has been quick to understand how social media can be adapted to suit their needs.

For decades, PR professionals and company press offices have issued press releases first by post, then via email. Now sites like Twitter, Google+ and Tumblr (www.tumblr.com) are perfectly placed as media to get your message across to a wide audience. In conjunction with a news feed, they are very quick, easy and cost-effective ways to broadcast information.

It's simply a case of filling in a short, catchy headline, then adding a shortened link to the URL where the press release is uploaded. The added advantage of issuing a release via Twitter is that it can be reposted several times, using slightly different wording, to ensure that the message resonates – something that might traditionally be regarded as overkill.

More and more press offices as well as PR agencies are now migrating their press release distribution onto social media, either directly or using third party companies such as Cision (http://us.cision.com/press-release-distribution/social-media-distribution.asp).

Air France (www.airfrance.info) has a dedicated bilingual Twitter feed (@AFNewsroom), which it uses as its news distribution channel, as distinct from its customer service Twitter account, @airfrancefr.

As well as a news distribution platform, social media are also a very effective way to communicate messages about brands.

The vast majority of journalists, as well as traditional media outlets, are now active on social media, particularly on Twitter, LinkedIn and Google+, and will be monitoring what is being distributed online, looking for stories and case studies.

Case study: Greater Manchester Police

One of the most effective recent examples of using social as a PR tool was by Greater Manchester Police. Faced with budget cuts approved by the government, the force wanted to communicate to politicians and the media how much work they were having to deal with. Police officers posted updates on three different Greater Manchester Police Twitter feeds (@gmp24_1, @gmp24_2, @gmp24_3) for 24 hours. Over this period, the police Twitter page (@gmpolice), which was also being displayed on the force's website, was updated with 3,205 tweets.

This one-day campaign attracted extensive interest from both print and broadcast media, leading to a debate in the press, all of which served to raise the profile of the force and highlight the difficulties they would face if their budget was cut – and helping to raise brand awareness about Greater Manchester Police in the process.

Brand awareness and establishment

Social media is the perfect arena in which to build or establish a brand. Until the advent of social networking sites, the only way companies could communicate their brand online was via their website – a one-dimensional tool that might be little more than a corporate e-brochure. In addition, reaching a mass audience required huge advertising budgets which were beyond the reach of all but the largest corporations.

Now, in conjunction with their website (or, for a few consumer-facing businesses, without a website), organisations can create a much more varied and multi-dimensional presence.

It is important to move away from thinking about a single online presence and look at multiple sites, as you can never be sure how you can reach the maximum possible audience. Using one or more of the social media channels enables companies to reach the widest number of people. And in some cases, if the content they are posting strikes a chord, there is always the possibility of it going viral – and potentially reaching millions of people.

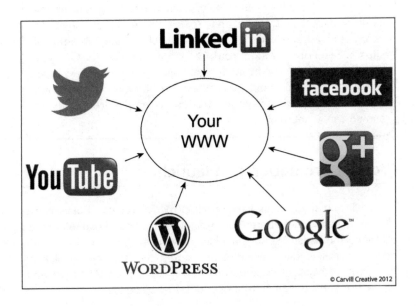

© Carvill Creative 2012

Armed with good-quality content, a comprehensive engagement strategy and an understanding of your target markets, it is possible to punch way above your weight.

Clearly global corporations such as Coca-Cola, Starbucks, Benetton, Mercedes-Benz and Amazon automatically have a high profile on social media, simply because they are established brands offline. However, they still use sites like Facebook and YouTube to reinforce their brands, engage with their communities and reach out to potentially new audiences. At the same time, they save millions of dollars in TV advertising by using their own channels, giving rise to the expression 'social TV' (see this *Forbes* article: http://onforb.es/QFnfet).

However, small businesses and start-ups can equally use social media to build their brands. Hitherto obscure artists such as Lily Allen and Ed Sheeran have achieved prominence by using social media; and companies have done the same. Take Sprinkles Cupcakes (www.facebook.com/sprinkles), who have built their brand almost entirely around Facebook and now have almost 77,000 engaged fans.

Visual organisations can really benefit from using sites like YouTube, Facebook, Pinterest and Flickr (www.flickr.com) as a way of showcasing what they do, while professional service-orientated brands can use Twitter, Google+ and LinkedIn, as well as blogs, as a fantastic way of providing regular insight and information to their customer base.

Case study: Chobani

Chobani (http://chobani.com), a Greek yoghurt maker based in New York State, have successfully taken on the giants of the industry, including Danone and Yoplait, by using social media to create awareness about their brand. Using the full array of sites – Facebook, Twitter, YouTube, Flickr, Foursquare, Google+ and Pinterest – they have a highly engaged online presence. Read more here about how they did it: www.fastcompany.com/1808071/chobani-yogurt-tickles-tastes-pinterest-addicts-and-so-can-your-brand.

Product promotion and launch

It is a fallacy that you cannot sell on social media. You can, but you have to employ methods that are more reflective of inbound marketing than traditional methods of selling. In addition, with paid-for advertising methods on social media – whether sponsored tweets, pay-per-click on Facebook or highlighted posts on Tumblr – it is possible to get your product or service right in front of your target audience.

The key is to engage with your target audience and slowly build momentum around your brand using a variety of social networks and high-quality content.

As authors, we are well aware of the power of social media to promote this book and indeed are using @BOBSthebook on Twitter to drive traffic to our book's website, www.thebusinessofbeingsocial.co.uk.

Here is a great blog from US-based digital and social media solutions company BarnRaisers that highlights some excellent product promotion campaigns on social: http://barnraisersllc.com/2011/12/12-case-studies-prove-roi-social-media-coupons.

Launches can also be made far more exciting using the full array of social media sites. Twitter hashtags, live tweets, streamed videos on YouTube and updates on Facebook give much greater depth to events.

An excellent example of this is Burberry, who use Twitter very effectively at fashion shows to launch their latest products (www.twitter.com/Burberry).

Gathering support for a cause

Few people can have missed the 'Arab Spring' that began in late 2010. The chain of events that led to the eventual overthrow of President Mubarak of Egypt was largely down to the creation of a Facebook Page (www.facebook.com/elshaheeed.co.uk) by Wael Ghonim, a Google employee. Acting as a conduit for dissent in Egypt and the wider region, this Facebook Page, along with other forms of social media, rallied people to a cause in a way that would not have been possible in the pre-social media age.

Charities can also make full use of social media to build their presence and gather support. American children's charity Champions for Kids (www.championsforkids.org) has used Twitter and Facebook as a way of magnifying the work of their marketing team and to reach out to communities around the USA.

Clearly, it has always been possible to ask for signatures on a petition to gather support, but the use of social media has transformed the way in which charities and not-for-profit organisations can get their messages across and help build momentum.

We are now in an age when everyone has a voice and every charity fundraising participant can promote themselves and their Just Giving (www.justgiving.com) page via social networks.

Indeed, social networking channels can provide many charities and non-governmental organisations (NGOs) with the publicity they may otherwise be unable to afford. Mobilising teams of volunteers to act as 'buzz market-ers' (marketing through word of mouth) can dramatically amplify the effec-tiveness of any campaign. Spreading messages virally through the social networks, as happened in the Middle East in 2010 and beyond, has a powerful effect – it just needs to be harnessed properly.

Humanising your brand: P2P

Everyone is familiar with the terms B2B (business to business) and B2C (business to consumer). Now we're in a *P2P* – people to people – age. From the dawn of civilisation, people have always dealt with people. The only thing that has changed over time is the technology and how it is used.

Ironically, many brands have moved away from the person-to-person human element with their online presences. Faceless websites that don't include members of staff, promotional materials that don't men-tion the human beings behind the brand and bland mission statements only serve to alienate potential customers.

In a society where any of your customers has a voice to praise or harm your brand using social media, it is important that we return to old-fashioned customer service.

At the same time, future customers want to know who they are doing business with – they are more interested in the human beings who are serving them than they are in your brand.

Search for any service on Google and you will get a host of websites offering much the same thing, with very little to differentiate between them. A key unique selling point (USP) for organisations must be the people who work there. So why not showcase them using LinkedIn profiles, blogs and videos?

Remember, any organisation is the sum of the people who work there, so why not play on this? For example, by listing the LinkedIn profiles of employees in your organisation, you are providing a more illuminating snapshot than any corporate brochure or website.

Case study: Innocent

Innocent put a real emphasis on portraying themselves as a com-pany run by humans for humans. From their website (www.inno-centdrinks.co.uk) to their array of social media sites, they highlight the people who work at the company, explain what they do and provide insights into their job as well as their daily lives. All of which helps to build the overall brand of an organisation.

Networking

Using Twitter is like attending the ultimate business conference that runs 24/7, 365 days a year, with millions of people having thousands of different conversations. LinkedIn, on the other hand, is like the ultimate business reunion where everyone you have ever met in your professional life – who you like (!) – is in one room.

According to the *Oxford English Dictionary*, networking in the business sense is defined as 'interacting with others to exchange information and develop professional or social contacts'. Social media provide the perfect conditions for doing this.

As well as LinkedIn, Facebook and Twitter, other social networks such as Google+, Tumblr (www.tumblr.com) and Quora (www.quora.com) plus, of course, blogging sites such as WordPress (www.wordpress.com) and Blogger (www.blogger.com), all provide an environment where people can communicate with each other online.

However, the two most popular sites for business networking are Twitter and LinkedIn. It is possible to use these channels to strengthen existing relationships as well as build brand new ones.

Ivan Misner, the founder of Business Networking International (www.bni.com) came up with the VCP model: **V**isibility + **C**redibility = **P**rofitability. This is as true of online networking as it is of face-to-face networking. The more visible you are, the more credible you become. The more credible you become, the more likely it is that people will want to do business with you.

On LinkedIn, 'groups' act almost like micro social networks where specialists can engage with each other. Whether you want groups about retail management, cat grooming, molecular biology or independent restaurant owners, it is possible to 'meet' like-minded people who work in the same field as you or could connect you to your chosen target audience. Google+'s circles are a similar way of communicating with and staying visible within specific networks of people. And on Twitter, by creating lists of suppliers or introducers it is possible to stay informed about what these people and/or businesses are doing.

As in normal face-to-face networking, it is important to establish who you wish to talk to/communicate with and to understand the rules of engagement and what content you wish to provide to these target audiences.

Business intelligence

Understanding your target audiences and gaining valuable business intelligence has never been simpler for organisations. There is a huge wealth of information online, whether posted by companies themselves or comments that others have posted in blogs, tweets or updates.

After corporate websites, company profiles on LinkedIn are often the first port of call to find information on organisations. Indeed, recruiters, competitors, journalists and students can often elicit more valuable data than they would from other sources.

On Twitter, it is possible to capture conversations about key brands and products. At the same time, by putting all competitors into private lists, companies can gain valuable market understanding about those organisations.

From recruiters using Facebook to get background information on candidates to potential suppliers checking out branded YouTube channels for corporations in order to understand how to communicate more effectively with them, social media can provide a huge amount of data.

Thought leadership

Blogs and social media provide a great medium for people to build their personal brands. Authors, artists, industry leaders and politicians all use a combination of channels to raise their profiles.

Acting as a metaphorical soap box, these channels give individuals the opportunity to raise their credibility, improve their visibility and communicate with their audience, in much the same way as companies do.

Celebrities have appropriated the power of the social networks to reach their fans across the world: indeed, in their own field, they are aiming to become 'thought leaders', whether in music, art, film or fashion. And increasingly, their fans wish to have a conduit through which they can communicate with their heroes.

In the corporate world, it is also becoming increasingly important for CEOs and leading people in professions to have some form of online 'voice'. Customers, clients and stakeholders are interested to hear their thoughts, in much the same way that journalists seek out opinion formers when writing about certain subjects in the traditional media.

Using social media channels in conjunction with blogs effectively enables individuals to reach audiences they would otherwise not have had access to.

From political bloggers such as Guido Fawkes (@GuidoFawkes) to business commentator Jack Welch (@jack_welch), and from leading environmental activists like Al Gore (@algore) to thought leaders such as Jack Dorsey (@jack), Twitter is a quick and easy way to get your message across.

On LinkedIn, the 'Update' box (which uses the same 140-character limit as Twitter) can be employed in a similar way to promote your blogs, videos or newsletters to your network of connections, while YouTube channels can add a much more human element to your personal brand.

Social media marketing action plan

- Think about your own organisation's business objectives.
- Then work out how you can use the social networks to meet these objectives.
- You may well be able to use one social network for a variety of purposes: for example, Facebook could be used for customer service and corporate and social responsibility; or you may need two separate Facebook Pages.
- Compile a grid showing the different social media channels on one axis and the various ways they can be used on the other axis. This will help you to see where they fit in your own organisation.
- Start small. You might consider using social media for one thing only. Get this right before expanding into other channels or trying to meet a plethora of different objectives.
- Keep updated with the latest developments in social media to stay ahead of the game.

3 | Content is king

What you will learn from this chapter:

- You are what you share
- Creating a content strategy
- Content vehicles
- Blogging tips
- The importance of keywords
- Unlocking the content potential in your business

You are what you share

The social media marketing channels we explore in this book, such as Twitter, Facebook, LinkedIn, Blogs, YouTube and the others covered in Chapter 10, present you with opportunities to share your content and get your messages across. However, now more than ever, *what* you share has never been more important. These channels have the potential to be far-reaching, extending beyond your usual 'databases', as they present opportunities for advocacy. If people love what they've read, seen or heard, they can share the content on their networks too, helping a wide audience to get to know about you, like you, trust you, share your messages and ultimately, even do business with you. And, of course, this isn't an onerous task; it's simply a case of hitting a button – like, share or retweet.

Given how potentially far-reaching the social media platforms can be, you need to ensure that you are not wasting the opportunity these channels provide by talking about the cheese sandwich you've just eaten. (Unless, of course, you're Pret A Manger and it's a tactic you've employed to showcase a new product!)

Businesses of all shapes and sizes need to get their 'content house' in order.

Ask yourself . . .

- Have you got a strategy for regularly creating fresh and acceptable content that meets specific business objectives?

- Have you got a blog that you regularly update for your business?
- Do you regularly create videos for your business – how-to videos, sharing FAQs, customer testimonials, new product and service features?
- Have you got any research information that others would be interested in? Could it be turned into an ebook and provide potential for data capture?
- Are you a leading authority in a specific area? Can you create 'white papers' or industry reports?
- Do you have interesting infographics that capture a subject perfectly?

Content is all around you, from your websites to service standards, internal training, product demos, new products, etc., so you need to ensure that you have a mechanism for collating the content in your business so that you can leverage it effectively.

Reasons why content is king

Fresh and compelling content is key for a number of reasons.

- **It helps you get found online.** Regular, fresh content is great for SEO (search engine optimisation) purposes. The more fresh and relevant content you provide, the more the search 'spiders' (so named because of 'the web') know that they can come to you and they will find updated, keyword-enabled content.
- **It keeps your online presence fresh.** Do you have any old news articles on your site? What's the date of your latest blog post – January 2011? Or even 2010? If so, how does that look to those reading your blog or visiting your website? Keeping your content fresh shares a really positive message about your business. And in an age where people search out products and services online and make decisions in just a few seconds, it's important that you appear up to date.
- **It grows trust and authority.** The content you create gives you something credible to shout about. The offline networking model VCP (outlined in Chapter 2) also fits with how people get to know you online. If you regularly share relevant and compelling content, you will grow a positive reputation. If you regularly share a load of spam links and promotional guff, ask yourself just how engaging or compelling that appears.
- **It grows brand awareness and reach.** As we mentioned at the start of the chapter, social media marketing channels can be far reaching – you just don't know where your content will end up and who will end up reading it. It may get picked up and shared in a very 'viral' way, growing awareness in ways that traditional media simply can't compete with.

- **It showcases the expertise and personality of the business.** Whether you are formally leveraging content in this way for thought leadership, or want to show a more human side of the business, what you communicate to the outside world creates an impression.

Of course, if you have a content strategy in place, there's also the opportunity of safeguarding what others are saying in your business. You can clearly set boundaries as to what is and what is not shared. Of course, content is best when it's authentic and transparent. However, you certainly don't want to be sharing content that is potentially damaging to your brand!

Why content matters so much

Once upon a time all an organisation had to worry about was its website presence.

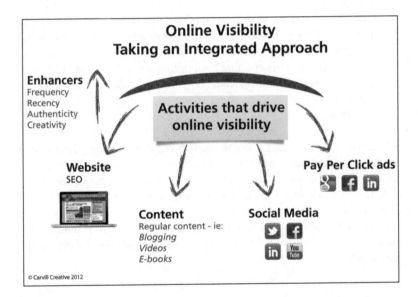

You need to ensure that your website content is regularly updated and refreshed – to maximise SEO efforts – but if you choose to participate on Facebook, Twitter, LinkedIn, YouTube, Pinterest, Google+ (and any vertical or social networks of the many that exist – more on that in Chapter 10), you need to be aware that these channels are all very content hungry.

Let's take a look at the four key channels from a content perspective.

1. **Twitter:** You are what you tweet. Whether you are retweeting someone else's content or showcasing your own, you need to have

clear objectives and policies and to ensure that the content is on message. In addition, the frequency is high: Twitter is a fast and fluid platform, so you could be posting ten or more updates a day. So what are you going to talk about?

2. **Facebook:** You are what you share. Whether you are advocating someone else's content or sharing your own, it needs to compel others to engage with it – to like, to share, to comment. One or two status updates a day still seem to gain more engagement than posting more than three a day on Facebook. However, you still need to be thinking about the content that engages this audience. Two updates a day is still 14 a week. (And, yes, weekends count.)

3. **YouTube:** You are looking for people to rate, like and share your video content. You may have the resources to create regular video content or you may be using apps like Animoto to turn presentations and images into video. YouTube is potentially the most resource-hungry medium of them all. If you plan out your video content, film 14 videos in one day and push out one a week, you will be filming three months' worth of content in one session. And doing that quarterly.

4. **LinkedIn:** You want to share status updates with your connections that compel them to share and engage with you. You may be able to leverage some of the content you share to Twitter and Facebook here. However, it may be that the content you are pushing to Facebook and Twitter isn't relevant for your professional connections. Again, you need to think about which content you serve to which audience.

We often find that 'traditional marketing messages' are pushed into these conversational channels: 'The content for traditional campaigns is already being created – so let's just push it across to our social channels too.' If the content fits and is relevant to the channel, this practice is perfectly acceptable. However, many traditional campaigns lead with a much more promotional element, so it may be that your messaging needs to be repositioned into a more conversational tone for the social platforms.

Developing a content road map

A couple of things we often hear when consulting or working with clients are, 'What do we talk about?' and 'We've run out of things to say.' Our response is that magical but simple mantra, 'Plan, Listen, Analyse – before you Engage.' If you've done all the planning and listening before you engage, you will either have a whole suite of content ready to roll, or you will have built a process of consistently developing content to feed the hungry channels in a targeted and purposeful way.

Let's take a look at some of the ingredients you could build into a content road map for your organisation.

1 Content audit

What content do you already have, and what content are you missing? Do some 'listening' to figure out what information gaps there are that you can fill. Customer pain points and problems are often a good starting point as you can then create useful content around purposeful solutions. Do the research and build up a list of topics around which to create content. Run a survey; listen to what people are saying (Twitter is a great resource for this); watch your analytics and see which pages people visit on your site; find out the questions customers most often ask your customer service team, chat services or online enquiries. Watch what competitors are doing and, which is important, watch the engagement levels of the information you are sharing. Very quickly you will start to pick up which topics resonate.

2 Content topics

Focus on business objectives to decide on key content themes and messages. Create a topic list, ideally focused on audience need. It could be that there are seasonal elements to the topic you wish to create. For example, an accountancy firm could consider tax seasons and certain business accounting deadlines throughout the year. So think about seasonality, if relevant, when creating your topics – just as a features editor would when putting together a year's content schedule for a magazine or journal.

3 Content collation

Now you know what you need, and you have a list of potential content topics, it's time to start pulling your content together. If relevant, work with different departments in the organisation to procure relevant content, and get them involved in regularly sharing information that can be leveraged for useful content and insights. Sharing your expertise is likely to be compelling content. And if you don't have the content in house, or the ability to create the content (e.g. if you think you require a professional team to create video content), consider whether you need to bring in resources to help you create it.

4 Content tone of voice and policies

As you are creating content, it's important to determine clear guidelines about what can and can't be communicated. Is it okay to mention competitors' or clients' names? What style or tone of voice do you adopt? A casual conversational tone works really well on blogs and Facebook, but if you're creating a white paper or research analysis, you may need to use a more formal business tone. Ensure that these elements are clear so that those creating and sharing the content have clear guidelines to work within.

5 Publishing schedule

With content creation in place, and tone of voice clearly understood, you now need to decide what and when you publish. Creating a timeline (e.g. weekly, monthly, annually) of when to publish your content is a useful exercise and you can make it as detailed as you wish.

You might want to create publishing schedules for different networks (a publishing matrix), focusing on frequency for each platform, for example:

- Twitter: 6–8 posts a day
- Facebook: two posts a day
- LinkedIn: three posts a week
- YouTube: one video a week.

You could even take the matrix further by including specific topics for each medium to focus on each week.

If you are dealing with audiences overseas, you may also want to consider the hour of day you publish your content to ensure optimum visibility during overseas business hours.

Keep your content interesting

Think about traditional media – magazines and newspapers – and the type of content they include. And, of course, think about news websites such as the BBC, Bloomberg or El País. A common theme is that they are a blend of media:

- videos
- articles
- images
- stories
- blogs
- FAQs
- expert advice
- tips and tactics
- webinars
- podcasts

- case studies
- Q&A sessions
- interviews
- polls and surveys.

When developing your content road map, think about these different media and what you could create, and how you can leverage each medium.

For example, you might take ten FAQs and create ten blogs or ten videos around these subjects. You could then create a podcast or a video blog. Or indeed a case study-style story to get a key point across. You could then tweet the blogs and video links and include relevant images, stories and videos on your Facebook Page; or ask questions and gauge audience feedback by running a poll or survey around the topic and, if relevant, push this poll across to your LinkedIn connections too.

You can see how you can 're-use' the same content in different ways, targeting it slightly differently according to the medium.

The power of blogging

Blogging is probably one of the simplest and most common methods organisations regularly use to communicate a more 'human' side of their business. A blog is a perfect mouthpiece for sharing a variety of content. Whether it's a video, an article, a case study or a story, a blog enables multimedia to be communicated in a regular and consistent way.

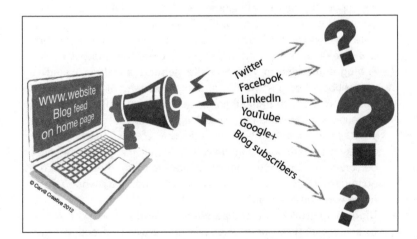

So, given that a blog is the most common form of content creation for organisations, let's take a good look at blogging. Before we get started, let's cover some essential blogging terminology.

- **Blog:** short for 'web log', a blog is a personal or company online journal. Others can participate – comment or share – one to many.
- **Post:** an article that has been published on a blog. You post a blog post, just as you would post a letter.
- **Category:** a blog category is simply a way of grouping posts that share a common theme. You can categorise posts into relevant sectors, e.g. social media, marketing, content management, online advertising, etc.
- **Blogging platform:** there are a number of platforms, some self-created, that form part of a website's content management system. Open source platforms such as WordPress, Blogger or Typepad (and there are many others) are more commonly used.

Now we've covered the terminology, let's get into the details of blogging.

Why blog?

- **Blogging enables you to say more.** It's a freer communication tool – and far more conversational – than many of the traditional media. Very often businesses find it difficult to share their brand message continuously or personally through visual advertising and traditional media, so blogging provides more insight into what that person, business or brand stands for, effectively sharing a more human voice of the business.
- **You can share authentic content on social platforms.** As we explored earlier in the chapter, you are what you share. Therefore, it's important that, as a business or brand, you have a good pot of authentic content to share with others. What better way to advocate what you do than to blog about it and share with others to grow awareness and opinion from those who potentially matter?
- **A blog embedded in your website generates traffic.** A study by www.hubspot.com showed that companies who blogged achieved 55% more website traffic than those that didn't. This makes sense because you are sharing something that drives people back to your site to read it. A blog embedded in your website gives your audience something to engage with. After all, many websites aren't designed as two-way communication portals; they are usually quite passive. So a blog (and indeed other social networks) enable a two-way conversation.
- **Blogs help grow brand and personal authority.** A blog enables you to share expertise about what you do, growing advocacy, awareness and authority for your brand or business as a thought leader in a particular area.

- **They entertain and grow 'fans'.** If people enjoy what you write, they will in time grow fond of your musings. Keep them entertained and they will share with others and ultimately you will develop a following. The more 'fans' you create, the more opportunity you have for advocacy and broadening your reach.

These are some great reasons for blogging, so let's now look at some tactical and practical blogging tips.

1. **Keep your blogs brief** (ideally about 500–700 words). But you can mix it up. Have a look at Seth Godin's blog (www.sethgodin.com). Some of his posts are literally two sentences. Others are two pages. But remember, you have to keep the audience engaged, and concise is usually best.
2. **Vary the topic.**
    o *Factual* – could focus around a recent change in legislation and implications, or a highly topical theme.
    o *Useful and practical* – ten tips, five steps to understanding ABC. People tend to enjoy 'quick tip'-style blog posts. But don't write every post in that style.
    o *Entertaining* – light and humorous so that the user understands that while you know your stuff, you're not taking life too seriously (if that fits with your overall tone of voice, of course).
    o *Opinion-driven* – asking for viewpoints from your audience. This is our view – what's yours? Do you agree, disagree?
3. **Watch yor splling and grammer.** Errors can really hinder credibility. Be sure to take advantage of spell-checking tools and brush up on your grammar. (*The Elements of Style* by William Strunk is a useful reference tool.)
4. **Use images** in a post to break up the text and add some relevant interest. Check out www.flickr.com, www.istockphoto.com or www.fotolia.co.uk for some low-cost yet good-quality shots. If you use images from Flickr, be sure to follow the guidelines and cite the reference in your posts.
5. **Consider video blogs.** You could consider turning your content into a 30- to 90-second video (short and to the point). Check out apps such as www.animoto.com, which is really useful for taking images and turning them into great video.
6. **Create attention-grabbing headings.** You should write the headline imagining that the user won't even see the article. So the headline has to grab attention and tell the story.
7. **Headline tips:**
    o *Question:* 'Would you let a marketer extract your teeth?' or 'Which test do you think got the most results?'
    o *How to:* 'How to get everyone to do what you want'
    o *Curiosity:* 'LinkedIn smarter than Facebook' (this piece was actually about photos on LinkedIn, where people were clearly

more smartly dressed than in the more casual pictures on Facebook

   ○ *Command:* 'If you read one thing today – read this'
   ○ *Quantify:* 'Twenty reasons you should do X'; 'Eight essential blogging tips you can't live without'.

8. **Use keywords** where you can – both in headers and throughout the content of the article. For example, 'Tax Planning Tips to blow your mind'.

9. **Schedule.** Stick to a tight publishing schedule. Blogging pays off over time – it's a marathon rather than a sprint and it takes time to build up relevant and optimised content. Ideally, blog at least three times a week.

10. **Insert a 'call to action'**, such as subscribe to the blog or to a newsletter, download our free guide, or get in touch.

11. **Promote your blog.** Promote links to your blog on your website and in email footers, business cards and other relevant offline and online marketing materials.

12. **Share your blog on relevant news services.** Search other relevant blogs in your sector and see what scope there is for you to post your blogs on other portals. For example, www.businesszone.co.uk encourages bloggers to share their blogs. And there are many other portals that enable you to do so. Search out those that are relevant for your business and start sharing.

13. **Share on social media.** Get your blog noticed by publishing links on social media vehicles such as Twitter, Facebook and LinkedIn (all social spaces relevant to your industry). And **make sharing simple**. Ensure that your blog has the 'sharing widgets' embedded.

14. **Write for the web.** Remember, people don't read online, they scan. Use short paragraphs. Short sentences. Bullet points. Clear headers.

15. **Be useful.** Try to provide at least one piece of practical 'how to' advice in each blog post. That way the reader will learn that you are always going to provide something useful.

16. **Don't push.** Don't focus your posts on selling your products or users will switch off (as they do in other conversational platforms like Twitter and Facebook). Instead, share advice, news and information that will prove useful to your readers (and grow your authority in the space).

17. **Be creative** in procuring your content. If you have published materials offline, 'blogify' them where relevant.

18. **Follow the leader.** If you find a respected and popular blogger/expert who focuses on areas you are interested in, your business area, subject, etc., write a post commenting on their post.

19. **Guest blog.** Ask others to guest blog on your blog and advise other blogs you respect that you'd be happy to do the same.

20. **Create a blog sign off.** Create a succinct sign-off sentence that describes your business, the author and includes a link back to your site.
21. **Link to other posts.** Refer to other posts you've written and include links so that you showcase other relevant and related content in your blog. (There are many plugins you can add to your blog that automate this process; for example on WordPress check out the 'Related Posts' plugin.)

Now you're armed with some tactical tips, you're ready to get started. So let's look at . . .

Types of blog posts to get you started

- **News articles.** These are the bread and butter of most companies' blogs. News articles could include industry news, company news, information for staff and anything new that is going on.
- **Case studies** make brilliant blog posts as they will help to sell your business. They will help visitors to your blog decide whether they want to do business with you and can lead to an increase in enquiries.
- **List posts.** People always like to read list posts, for example 'The top 10 reasons to avoid . . .' or 'The five best ways to . . .'
- **Stories.** People love a good story, especially if it's witty and they can relate to it. Think of any funny or poignant business stories you might have with a meaningful message. (There's more on stories later in this chapter.)
- **FAQ posts.** If you are constantly fielding questions on a particular subject, or want to help people find the answer to a question, FAQ posts are a very good idea. Think of the top five most-asked questions and start there.
- **Employee spotlight.** One way of engaging with and rewarding your employees is to spotlight one each month. You could interview them or praise them for work they have been carrying out via a blog article.

Whether you are setting off alone or creating a corporate blogging team – here's your checklist:

What now?

- Appoint an editor (that may just be you!).
- Create an editorial/features list.
- Brainstorm some headlines.
- Create an editorial process/content/images/style.
- Allocate blog posts.

- Set aside an hour to blog each week/month.
- Set alerts in Outlook or on your phone to remind you.
- Be conversational and be yourself (don't be too formal).
- Keep at it.

Remember . . .

Blogging is a marathon, not a sprint. It's unlikely to be an overnight success, so give it time and keep at it.

The importance of keywords when planning content

As a consumer it's likely that when you are looking for a new product or service you turn to Google or another search engine (maybe even Twitter, Facebook and LinkedIn) and hit their search bars with some all important 'keywords' – or sometimes a 'key phrase'. For example:

- social media consultancy London
- online advertising advice Tucson Arizona
- parapluies verts Marseilles.

When people search online, they use just a few keywords to find what they are looking for. Therefore, if you want to be found by those seeking your products and services, it's important that you provide a consistent and optimised presence online across all the portals that you are represented on (website, Facebook, blog, Twitter, Google+, LinkedIn, YouTube, etc.).

Keywords are the 'DNA' of your business. They are of paramount importance for:

- search engine optimisation
- online social platform profiles
- news feeds
- website content
- tweets
- Facebook Page updates
- tagging YouTube videos
- pay-per-click campaigns
- building communities on social media
- LinkedIn Profiles.

Throughout this book we emphasise the importance of using keywords to optimise your profiles and status updates. Discovering your keywords is key, so let's take a look at ways of exploring and determining your keywords.

Discovering your keywords

When you created your website, you will ideally have engaged an SEO expert or team to ensure that your website platform would be as optimised as possible for web searches.

The SEO team would be fully conversant with keywords and would (usually) have undertaken a keyword exercise to identify your keywords in order for them to populate your website with relevant information.

Other less scientific methods you may wish to explore include the following.

- Ask your colleagues and business associates to list the top five words that apply to your business.
- Ask your customers to do the same (How did you find us? Which words did you type into a Google search to find us?). This could be a manual or automated process.
- Look at Google Analytics to see what keywords people use. If you have Google Analytics running on your site, you can review the keywords people have used to find you, following this route:
  - traffic sources
  - sources
  - referral
  - search
  - organic.
- This will show you a list of the words, in order of relevance, that people have used to find your services. Undertake this process regularly to watch for any shifts in keyword trends.
- Use Google's Keyword Tool to find the most popular searches around your products or services. If you are stuck for ideas, Google's Keyword Tool offers you a free resource to explore. The tool provides you with traffic information related to specific keywords, so you might want to experiment with specific keywords to see if you gain more traction by optimising your content with high-traffic keywords that are relevant to your product or service.

Keep monitoring keyword activity via Analytics and keyword tools so that you are continually optimising.

You may want to optimise different facets of your business with different keywords, so explore and be consistent across your content in line with your specific objectives.

Make your communications count

Clearly, one way to make your communications count is to ensure that they are keyword optimised. However, while you want to optimise your content so that it's leveraged for search engines, first and foremost you are writing to engage people.

Experts agree that when you are promoting your services and writing your email, sales letter or website promotional material, Facebook update, etc., the key activity is to 'plan your writing'. Ninety per cent of the thinking should happen before those eager fingers start tapping at the keypad.

The focus of your communication is to grow 'share of mind', to get people to know you, like you, trust you – and, ultimately, do business with you. So let's take a look at some elements you need to consider when crafting your communications.

- **Focus on the objective.** What's the end game? Ask yourself the question, 'What do I want my communication to achieve?' Consider this and then work backwards, asking yourself key questions such as, 'How do we best communicate that?' Simply put, start with the end in mind.
- **Be yourself.** Personalise the communication as much as you can and demonstrate a sound knowledge of your audience's business dynamics and needs as well as a clear understanding of the obstacles they face. If the reader believes that you have empathy with their situation they are far more likely to continue reading. Be human!
- **Don't talk too much about yourself.** Readers are far more interested in what you can do for them than they are in what you do. Focus on the opportunities and benefits your products and services offer them.
- **Use the words 'you' and 'your'** as much as possible and minimise 'we' and 'us'. This will warm up your communications considerably. Avoid words such as difficult, fail, failure, hard, loss, obligation, try, sold, worry, cost, bad, fail, lose, sold, worry. (Consumer psychology research has tested communications littered with such words and found that they have a negative impact on your audience.) Use positive words – such as results, discover, approve, deserve, easy, proven, save, trust, truth, understand, value and vital – when you can.
- **Use sub-heads**, bullet points and highlighted or underlined text to convey key points. Be sure that your key messages don't get lost in a sea of text.
- **Communicate a very clear proposition.** Have you seen the 'Dollar Shave' video? We love it for a number of reasons. It's humorous, it's simple; but, very cleverly, it gets the value proposition across very quickly. In the first sentence we hear 'I'm the founder of Dollar

Shave Club and for a dollar a month we'll send your razors straight to your door' – a very simple proposition, said very succinctly. Whether your medium is video, written, visual or auditory – keep the proposition simple.

- **Make it easy for people to engage.** Have clear 'calls to action' and very clear instructions and signposts as to what you want people to do. If it's a video, include your website URL or Facebook Page address at the end of the video (depending on where you want to send your readers). If you want them to download an ebook or guide, make the instructions very clear and simple to follow. If you want them to share something, include social sharing icons in obvious places. The more instructions you provide, and the simpler and clearer you make the instructions, the better.

Content that engages

Providing engaging content isn't just about making it simple for people to engage with your content. In today's information-rich world, we need to stand out from the crowd and create content that resonates with our audiences and compels them to share.

Stories have always created a strong human connection. From stories told round a campfire to being tucked up in bed listening to our parents read us the dark wonders of Hans Christian Anderson and the brothers Grimm, the engagement of storytelling is timeless.

When considering how to create content that compels others to share your content, and therefore amplify your message, another element to think of in your blend of content is the stories you can create about experiences around your products and services.

Let's take a look at some storytelling ideas.

- **Educate others about the range of solutions you provide.** You may already have FAQs or user manuals/guides in place, but they may be pretty dry and unappealing. Challenge yourself and/or your team to think about how you could create an educational story about your products or services. You could perhaps create a character who has a specific problem; you could write in dialogue or use an 'agony aunt' style. Whatever style you use, creating a story provides a warmer and more compelling tale than a dry list of FAQs that run on for pages and pages.
- **Share real-life examples of what's working for others.** Case studies are actually perfect stories. In a case study you have the opportunity to use real-life experiences, from both your perspective and the client's point of view. If the information is sensitive and your client does not want their name revealed, you can simply use a generic term instead, e.g. 'Cosmetic Dentist in east

London'. With a case study you can explain what was happening before your involvement, how you managed the project and the outcomes. A beginning, a middle and an end – the perfect structure for a successful story. You could also include a 'to be continued' element so that you can keep adding to the story as things progress further.

- **Share expertise and thought leadership.** Your opinion and viewpoint can be turned into a story. Let's say there's something really topical in the news or trending on social networks around which you can create a story. This enables you to share your personality and your viewpoint and showcase your experience and expertise in a specific area – thus growing your credibility as a thought leader.

You could interview someone, have a Q&A session or undertake a piece of research and build a story around that. These examples are just a few ways in which you can create compelling stories to share as part of your content strategy.

There are some wonderful bloggers you should think about following. We've mentioned him before, and we'll mention him again – Seth Godin is a great storyteller, and his daily blog is always widely shared. Why? For the very reason that he's sharing compelling, thought-provoking and educational stories.

A key message here is to get creative with your content creation opportunities. Don't hold back on how you can leverage storytelling in your social media marketing and content strategy. After all, as we've said a few times, you are what you share, so be sure to make your content as compelling as possible.

Social media marketing action plan

- Take an integrated approach to your visibility online.
- Develop a content road map.
- Use a mix of media.
- Understand the power of blogging.
- Think about the importance of keywords when planning and sharing content.
- Create a publishing schedule for content.

4 | Twitter

What you will learn from this chapter:

- The many uses of Twitter
- Practical set-up and getting started
- Profile set-up
- Day-to-day management
- Twitter trivia
- Dos and don'ts, etiquette, practical advice
- HR internal policies on Twitter
- Disclaimers
- Analytics – tools, TweetReach, Google Analytics, etc.

What is Twitter?

Put very simply, Twitter is a social networking service that allows the user to answer, in no more than 140 characters, the simple question, 'What are you doing?'.

When we started using Twitter, around four years ago, the tweets that people were sharing focused on answering that very question. Tweets such as 'I'm eating a cheese sandwich,' 'I'm just heading to the park to read a book,' 'Meeting up with Suzie at 3pm – heading there now' took up the majority of the Twitter airspace. And even we, number one Twitter advocates, watched the world of Twitter roll by, thinking 'What's the point of that?'

If you've been tweeting for a few years you will have noticed a seismic shift away from largely mundane tweets towards more focused, information-rich, useful and compelling ones. Many tweets now include live links directing people to articles, landing pages, offers, images, videos, websites and more, which means that they have become a fabulous tool for driving traffic and audiences to a specific event, whether that event is a blog post, a research paper, a picture or a video, etc.

Like most technologies, Twitter started off as one thing and evolved into something else. Why the shift? Well, the marketers woke up and realised that a shift in consumerism was upon us. Their customers, their target audiences, were happily chatting on Twitter, every day and for hours, so they realised that this was a potentially far-reaching communication channel that they could adopt.

Today, while many people still do use Twitter to talk about cheese sandwiches to their genuine friends, the channel has also been appropriated by businesses, communication teams, brands and marketers the world over who are leveraging the simplicity and scale of the platform in an often targeted and purposeful way.

The current picture

The appetite for Twitter is gathering pace. Twitter now has approximately 10 million users in the UK and around 200 million worldwide, and it continues to grow. By the time this book is published, these stats are likely to be out of date (you can review the latest statistics on our Business of Being Social blog), but the numbers are highly unlikely to have decreased.

One of Twitter's greatest assets (and there are many – we'll explore them in detail in this chapter) is the fact that each communication is short.

Messages, known as tweets, are limited to just 140 characters – so those who participate are having to become masters of saying more with less. In an age when we are saturated with information, the fact that messages are limited to short snippets of just 140 characters feeds our growing appetite to quickly assimilate an abundance of information. In effect, you can still listen to the noise, but it's easier to take what you need and ignore anything surplus to requirements.

Twitter works wonderfully with mobile

At the beginning of this book we talked about the growth of mobile technology as well as how mobile browsing and purchasing via mobile is on the increase (and destined to overtake desktop browsing by the end of 2013).

Twitter, with its 140-character tweet limit, works in harmony with mobile communications.

This is evidenced in the UK by the fact that it is now the fourth-largest country for Twitter users in the world, with 80% of users accessing Twitter via mobile phones.

Real time

Another key asset of Twitter is just how 'real time' the platform is. We often refer to Twitter as the 'Usain Bolt' of the social networks. In contrast to Facebook and LinkedIn, Twitter updates don't stick around for all that long. The sheer volume of tweets (approximately 400 million tweets per day) means that what you see in your Twitter stream changes rapidly. Within seconds a stream is populated with new tweets.

It's reported that the average lifetime of a tweet is approximately just 22 seconds. So this has significant impact on how you manage your communications in this fast-moving and real-time space.

Real-time feedback

A positive element of real time is the fact that you can listen in to conversations in real time too. Research programmes that previously may have taken weeks or months to pull together can be executed via Twitter, and they can enable a real-time understanding of impact and feedback as things actually unfold.

For example, in the autumn of 2012 the UK supermarket Waitrose ran a campaign on Twitter through which they wanted to engage their audience and learn the reasons why people love shopping at Waitrose. They posed the question: 'I love shopping at Waitrose because _____ ' #WaitroseReasons.

Whilst the campaign didn't go quite as they had expected, it did create a significant amount of free PR for the brand. (You can read more on this in a *Daily Mail* article: www.dailymail.co.uk/news/article-2205975/Waitrose-Twitter-backlash-I-shop-Waitrose—I-dont-like-surrounded-poor-people.html?ito=feeds-newsxml.)

Perhaps it would have been better to have given some 'steer' to this question rather than leave it so open. Had they said, 'We love shopping at Waitrose because the strawberries are super fresh and locally sourced – what do you love?', that could have steered the feedback along a 'food quality' direction, rather than keeping the questioning so broad that people could take it anywhere.

On Twitter, people are talking online and in real time. With the appropriate tools and know-how you can engage with an audience to ask questions and get real-time responses. You can also track keywords and be alerted to any specific conversations around those keywords. This is useful either for growing engagement and connecting with relevant people or simply for learning about views. So real time presents some key opportunities.

Uses of Twitter

Twitter is a hive of activity. It's the buzziest network of them all (so far) and its versatility makes it the must-have social media channel – it's a perfect vehicle for sharing, targeting, connecting and listening.

Such versatility means that even if a business doesn't actually want to engage via Twitter or have a formal presence on the site, Twitter can still be used as a research channel – for tracking conversations, brand mentions, sentiment and insights.

Let's take a look at some real-world uses for Twitter.

Customer support and service

A number of organisations now leverage Twitter as a key resource for customer support. Take a look at @BlackBerryHelp, for example. This support account regularly engages by tweeting tactics and tips in answer to questions. The account makes it clear when the support service is staffed and they also showcase the 12 people on their team who are responsible for managing the support Twitter account. Another support account to review is @XboxSupport. Its profile claims (true or not) to be the most responsive brand on Twitter. Again, the profile clearly shows when the support account is staffed and the team of 19 who are involved in the support service.

If you use Twitter for customer support (as we mentioned back in Chapter 2) you need to cover a few elements.

1 Speed of response

If you promote a support service, you really have to deliver. Even minutes can be too long to respond. Therefore, you have to be resourced effectively, both with tools to track the queries and with people ready and equipped to respond.

Social media story

One of our team needed a code to update a piece of antivirus software. It was a simple procedure, but they didn't have the code, so they went to the Symantec website. At the time, there were no signs of social media on the website, so the main point of contact for support queries was a phone number. A call was made and the button-pressing, navigating services and holding on began. They were held in a queue for about 40 minutes. Of course, they took to Twitter with the message, 'Arrgh Symantec – nightmare been on hold to support for 40 mins.'

It took just a few seconds before someone from @symantec responded: 'Hi – It's the support team here. How can we help?' Our team member advised them of the challenge, they came back with a link to a website which opened a chat session and the issue was resolved in just a few minutes.

Of course, we then went back to Twitter to praise their customer service efforts: '@symantec – Excellent use of Twitter for customer support. 5 Stars.'

Speed of response and having a mechanism and process in place to get us off the live channel and resolve the issue turned a negative experience into a very positive one – and one that was visible to all our followers too.

2 Get them off the platform

You really don't want someone ranting and raving on Twitter where all your followers can see. This may just spark negative feedback from others and before you know it, there's a barrage of insults building up. Therefore, be sure you have a mechanism in place (as Symantec did). For example, are you going to send people off to a chat page or ask them to call you or direct message you (a direct message can be seen only by the sender and receiver), as evidenced by the @TMobileUKHelp account? Or do you have a website link or a chat facility to send them to, or even a support number for them to call?

3 Setting expectations

The accounts mentioned above, and many support accounts on Twitter, say clearly when the support account is manned. If you say your support account is manned 24/7, you've got to deliver. (Perhaps that's what @XboxSupport are delivering on – whatever time it is, they will respond?) Setting expectations of when the account is staffed doesn't, however, always delight customers. A recent delegate from one of our training courses tweeted us to advise about poor customer service from @Waitrose. She had tweeted them on a Saturday evening and had not had a response and had therefore moaned at them. In fairness, their Twitter account clearly states: 'Follow us for all the latest news, recipes and offers from Waitrose. We're available on Twitter whenever our shops are open.' And clearly their shops were closed at the time she tweeted them, hence the lack of response. Even though Waitrose had clearly laid out the terms of their engagement, the delegate was still disappointed. She continued to tweet them and then brought in competitor supermarket chain Sainsbury's, who, unfortunately for Waitrose, were very responsive and engaged with the delegate regarding the question she had originally raised about 'freezing salmon'.

This is clear evidence that consumers expect to get a quick response via Twitter even when the company or brand has endeavoured to manage expectations – and further, that they will potentially switch allegiances to those that are listening and engaging.

4 Escalation and response policies

Always hope for the best but plan for the worst. It's important to at least plan some response measures for 'what happens if it all goes wrong' scenarios. Many of the #fails on Twitter (a hashtag commonly used when a person is sharing a gripe about a negative service issue) are largely down to the fact that effective planning and procedures haven't been put in place to deal effectively with complaints or unrest.

McDonalds ran a well-publicised campaign around the hashtag #McDStories, encouraging people to share their McDonalds stories. Like the #WaitroseReasons campaign, the call to action was much too broad and, of course, laid McDonalds wide open to receiving feedback about all experiences with the brand – the majority of which were not positive.

The PR team at McDonalds very quickly saw what was happening (there was a bit of 'bashtagging' going on) and removed the promoted hashtag. It eventually took about a week for the noise to die down (and we're sure it hardly made a dent in their huge brand), but with better planning they could have steered consumers down another path.

Many people were keen to see Waitrose's response to the #Waitrose Reasons campaign. Pretty quickly (within just a matter of hours) their PR team came out with their heads held high. They did the right thing. They very quickly thanked everyone for their responses, they were transparent and, in as many words, said, 'Well, that wasn't really what we were expecting – however, it's been a hugely illuminating exercise and one which we have learned a great deal from.'

If you are using Twitter for customer service, be sure to get your escalation policies and procedures in place – just as you would in the offline world. In a highly connected and potentially viral world, the way you manage complaints and challenges is absolutely key. Remember, people aren't necessarily looking for the answer there and then. They often just want to know that their voice is being heard and that someone will look into things and get back to them. Ignoring social communications (or any service-focused communications for that matter) is not the right thing to do. So be sure you have clear processes in place. Don't be stuck for words – be sure you have it all covered.

Brand reputation management

Many organisations we meet express this sentiment: 'I don't want our organisation to go on Twitter because what if someone says something awful about us?'. The truth of the matter is, whether your organisation is on Twitter or not people may still be talking about you – both positively and negatively. The question is, would you rather let them talk about you and have no idea what they are saying, and no means of talking back to them; or would you rather embrace what they are saying and perhaps join the conversation?

The fashion brand 'No Refunds Policy' case study in Chapter 2 is a classic example of missing out on what is being said about a brand. That case study shows that tracking your brand online can be most illuminating. (Chapter 8 on Listening will showcase a range of practical ways of listening out for and tracking brand mentions.)

Polling and product feedback

Twitter being so 'real time' means that it's a wonderful platform for gathering information quickly. For example, you may want to run a poll on a specific topic or get some feedback on a product or service.

A really neat and simple tool for running polls or surveys on Twitter is www.twtpoll.com. The great thing about Twtpoll (and that isn't a typo – there isn't an i), is just how simple it is to use. It also provides you with diagrams and pie charts illustrating the feedback and information about who said what. It's a useful tool not only for engaging your followers and potentially reaching new audiences, but also for content creation.

One good example of a great use of a Twtpoll was a university lecturer who polled his students to get a view on the order of their tutorials – they were voting on which modules they wanted to tackle first. But the options are endless.

Listening in, capturing conversations and sales leads

We've already mentioned that Twitter is a fast and noisy place. Millions of tweets are circulating at any one time. Cutting through the noise and tuning in to what's important to you is therefore key, otherwise it all becomes overwhelming and pointless. If you just get on Twitter and start talking, using the same promotional marketing speak as you might for traditional marketing messages, you just become part of the noise. It's not targeted, it's not purposeful and – guess what – it's unlikely that anyone's tuning in. Listening in and doing your research on what's being said by the people you are keen to engage with is fundamental. (More on Listening in Chapter 8.)

News distribution

Many businesses create regular newsletters or information to share with clients or prospective clients, helping them to stay in touch and keep up to date with what they're up to. Twitter provides a perfect vehicle for showcasing news and updates about recent business activity. Of course, you shouldn't simply fill your Twitter activity with all your own news – that would become pretty boring. But it's certainly a useful platform for sharing relevant news as well as keeping clients and prospective clients in touch with your activities.

Traditional PR activities can be leveraged by not only going through to all your usual traditional contacts, but by also sharing with relevant influencers on Twitter. Most credible journalists are now on Twitter, so it's also worth tracking down those journalists relevant to your sector, following them and sharing information with them via Twitter too.

Whatever news you have to share, whether you're promoting an event, launching a product, highlighting a PR activity or showcasing your monthly newsletter, think about how you can share the news in a relevant and targeted way on Twitter. For example, if you have a monthly newsletter that includes five articles, you could perhaps break those articles up into five different tweets rather than simply tweet the whole newsletter.

Brand awareness

Brands and businesses of all shapes and sizes are on Twitter and many of the larger brands, such as Coca-Cola and Innocent, are largely there to engage with their followers and for general brand building. Even though research identifies that people are more likely to follow other people on Twitter and that they are more likely to engage with a brand on Facebook, Twitter is still relevant for brand building and awareness.

If you are using Twitter for brand building, you need to consider the implications.

- What content shall we create?
- How shall we engage our followers?

Traditionally, brand building is largely about advertising spend and being as visible as possible. Extraordinarily innovative creative campaigns and breathtaking cinema advertisements get people talking – and those same 'buzz' principles apply to Twitter, even though you have only 140 characters to play with.

Nike and the 2012 Olympics

During the 2012 London Olympics, many of Nike's billboard, cinema and underground athlete advertising campaigns featured not a website address but a simple @address with the hashtag #makeitcount. Nike started the campaign in January 2012 encouraging everyone to make 2012 the year they would achieve – the year they would do better than they ever imagined. They posed the question,

'How will you make 2012 count?' Creative advertising and videos to support this were rolled out featuring powerful images of key sports people such as Mo Farah, Paula Radcliffe, Rio Ferdinand and others. The #makeitcount campaign was clearly aligned with the Olympics, even though Nike was not one of the official sponsors.

This campaign was a big branding exercise for Nike. It showed that they were aligned with key sports people who would be competing in the Olympics, and via the hashtag it had a clear execution on Twitter, where people could share and get involved in the conversation.

From superbrand to community charity

In contrast to the huge superbrand Nike, the Citizens Advice Bureau (CAB) ran a brand awareness campaign focused on chang-ing perceptions of what the CAB actually do.

Over the years, they had kept coming up against the same aware-ness challenge – the key perception the public has of the CAB is that it mainly provides advice about consumer complaints. In reality, the CAB – which is a charitable organisation – provides a whole range of advisory services, and it was clear that the general public were largely unaware of the diversity of advice and services avail-able from their local CAB.

Since it works to a tight budget, as many charities have to, one of the CAB offices wanted to grow awareness in the most cost-effective way. So it turned to Twitter. It launched a campaign branded with the hashtag #CABLive, which it promoted in various ways, not only to the general public, but also to other CABs in their region, thus amplifying the message and reach. The campaign focus was to take a week in March and tweet every incident it dealt with (including the #CABLive hashtag in every tweet). This activity demonstrated to its many followers the diversity of advice on offer.

The campaign was hugely successful – engagement levels grew and awareness of additional services was enhanced. It was so successful that it is going to be repeated by the regional branches involved and other branches too.

Gathering support for a cause

Many charities and causes use the power of Twitter to orchestrate a mass stance. For example, when police stations or services are being cut, people turn to Twitter to build awareness of the work they do.

The online lobbying organisation 38 Degrees (www.38degrees.org.uk – 'People, Power, Change') brings millions of people together to leverage the power of the crowd. They use their @38_degrees account to extend the scope of their online campaigns, amplify their messages and reach new audiences. They report their successes and keep their supporters engaged. And they encourage their supporters to share via Facebook and Twitter and get their friends involved too.

Case study: Hugh's Fish Fight

Another example is celebrity chef Hugh Fearnley-Whittingstall's campaign on overfishing. When a documentary about the overfishing issue was aired on Channel 4 in the UK, the hashtag #fishfight was promoted throughout the programme. People were encouraged to join his campaign on Twitter and Facebook and to sign up to his website. He now has over 250,000 Likes on Facebook and over 45,000 followers on Twitter, and almost a million people signed up to his online overfishing petition.

While the number of Likes or sign-ups to his website may dwarf the number of followers he has on Twitter, the campaign uses Twitter very wisely. Whenever Hugh needs to bring attention to some parliamentary debate or put pressure on MPs who are debating key issues, he reaches out on Twitter to his trusted fish fighters and asks them to tweet the relevant MP to advise that the fish fighters are watching and to encourage them to do the right thing.

The campaign continues to build a captive and targeted audience that he can draw upon when necessary (e.g. his recent prawn campaign to supermarkets). This just couldn't happen offline: it would be far too difficult to orchestrate that many people to respond at a specific time. However, a quick tweet and a quick press of a button to retweet it (share it with your audience) takes very little effort and adds significant impact. How is that MP going to feel if he or she receives 5,000 tweets advising them to do the right thing? Or how a supermarket would react to 38,000 tweets about its prawns?

Humanising your brand

People do business with people, and Twitter provides a perfect vehicle to showcase the people behind the brand. Like some of the support accounts we mentioned previously, many accounts show pictures of a number of the team and their different Twitter handles. (Your Twitter name – @name – is referred to in old Citizens' Band (CB) radio terminology as a 'handle'.)

Another key thing to consider is that we are now in an era in which using search engines to find products and services is the norm. As a consumer, it is highly likely that you now research items you're considering buying on Google or other search engines before you buy them.

The trust factor

As consumers in this 'always on' society, instead of hitting the high street or nearby shopping mall to find products and services, we now regularly check out our trusty mobile devices, whether a smartphone, tablet or laptop. We open the search engines (still usually Google) and search for products and services. When searching we insert the all-important keywords or a short key phrase we're looking for (for example 'chartered accountant Edinburgh') and await the results.

When we then click on a relevant link, we're hoping that the end of the journey fits with what we're looking for. If it doesn't it's no real problem, as there are lots of other choices we can click back to.

Example

Let's say you click on a link and find the following websites.

- **Site A** is a rather outmoded looking website. There is a blog feed on the home page, but the most recent piece of news is dated November 2010. Other than that there are no signs of life. Do we feel that we're going to get a great service or product from a site like this?
- **Site B** is a fast-loading and polished-looking website. On the home page there are social media icons advising us that we can 'join the conversation'. Not only is there a blog feed, where we can see the latest blog post – which is just a couple of days old – but there is also a Twitter feed pulled through, where we can see what they are sharing and talking about – and that they are clearly very much alive, as their latest tweet was just a few minutes ago.

Which site would you feel more inclined to do business with, A or B? For sure – it's B.

Targeting

Twitter is essentially a huge database. You have the ability to interrogate that database to find everyone you might wish to partner, network or engage with. Whether you are researching the key influencers in your sector, a specific target audience, ideal new business partners, advisers, peers, Twitter is a rich and open resource.

Admittedly, researching and targeting takes a bit of effort and time, but it certainly beats 'list purchasing' from data houses and then making cold contact. With Twitter, you can target influencers or audiences and then develop relationships with them – following them, sharing information with them, directing conversations to them – and ultimately, getting them to know you – like you – trust you – with the intention that they will ultimately do business with you.

Once you find a great contact, you can review who they follow and who is following them. You can review their lists (how they've segmented their followers) and see any lists that other Twitter users have put them into. This is a particularly useful feature, as someone may already have compiled a list of the types of people you are looking to connect with. (There's more on Twitter lists later in this chapter.)

Getting started with Twitter

Joining is really simple – visit www.twitter.com and register. But then we seriously suggest you pause for a while before you dive in. The geniuses behind Twitter have made it as simple and user friendly as possible to set up an account, but you need to do some all-important thinking before you get started.

Key terminology

We'll be using this terminology throughout the rest of the chapter. (Do check out the Social Media Glossary at the end of this book; and you can also visit the Social Media Jargon Buster at www.carvillcreative. co.uk.)

Twitter handle

Taken from the CB radio term 'handle', this is the @name – which is the all-important brand on Twitter. For example, @michellecarvill, @savvysocialDT and @carvillcreative are how we are found on Twitter, and they are effectively our brands on Twitter.

Retweet

Retweeting a tweet simply means forwarding it to all your followers. Twitter makes it easy for you to share something by retweeting it (often abbreviated to RT).

Favourite

To favourite (or favorite) a tweet is like 'bookmarking' it. When you favourite a tweet it sticks around in your Favourites log, which can be found in your Profile settings on the left-hand side of the screen.

Favourites can be really useful, for a number of reasons.

- To remind you of great articles you've found on Twitter.
- To keep positive testimonials about your brand, product or service, and showcase a link from your website saying 'See what people say about us on Twitter.'
- To have a themed repository, for example: 'See all the tweets about our latest campaign.'

To favourite a tweet, you simply hit the Favorite link and you'll see an orange star appear in the right-hand corner of the tweet you are 'favouriting'. To unfavourite something you simply click on the Favorite link again. When you favourite a tweet the initiator receives a message that it's been favourited.

Following

If you follow someone, you see their tweets. Therefore, the more people you follow, the more tweets you see. But unless they are following you they won't see your tweets.

If someone follows you, they see your tweets. And if you both follow each other you will both see each others' tweets.

Direct messaging

A bonus of two people following one another is that it gives you permission to take the conversation out of the public eye. The conversation stays on Twitter, but becomes one to one rather than one to many. You can send a direct message either by using the direct message function on Twitter – or by putting a 'd' instead of an @ sign before the Twitter name, e.g. 'd @michellecarvill' or just 'd michellecarvill' (both work) instead of @michellecarvill. (Note: you do need to leave a space after the d and before the handle.)

Following and unfollowing

When you find someone you want to follow, you click on the blue button on the right-hand side of their profile. When you click on that button it will switch to 'Following'. If you click the button again, it will switch to

'Follow'. Following or unfollowing someone is merely a matter of clicking a button.

Hashtags

The # can be used to categorise your tweet to a particular topic. People who search on Twitter for the topic that you are referring to will see your tweet. It's also used to promote an event or activity – TV programmes often use them to aggregate conversation around the specific programme or topic. Anyone can create a hashtag – it's simply a case of adding a # before any word or phrase: #hopethatmakessense! (We demystify hashtags completely later in this chapter – see page 78.)

What next?

Now we've covered some common terminology, let's look in some more detail at getting started. While the platform is very simple to set up, what you do with it is the all-important factor; so before you dive in, you really should consider the following.

Decide your objectives

You need to think about how you want to use Twitter – once you've started, it may be difficult to change tactics.

- Are you going to use it for general social interaction, or for business purposes?
- If the latter, what image do you want to portray?

Considering what you want to achieve from connecting on Twitter is vital to how you position yourself before you start.

Create a targeted profile

Once you've decided on your positioning you can set up your profile.

You can see from this profile overview that completing the fields is pretty simple. However, remember that your objectives steer exactly how you want to be positioned.

Let's say that you're an expert, award-winning cat groomer and your objectives on Twitter are:

1. to showcase your expertise, so that you become known as the 'go to' person about cat grooming issues
2. lead generation – listening in for people who may need your advice or your services, so that you can start networking with them, and encourage them to know you, like you, trust you and ultimately do business/engage with you.

When fixing your Twitter @handle would you call yourself @marybloggs or would you call yourself @catgroomer? If you call yourself @catgroomer, you have a good chance of being found when people are searching for cat groomers on Twitter. Also, your proposition is very clear. You don't have a cryptic brand that will be hard for someone to figure out what it is you do.

Your @handle can be changed at any time

You could start off with one @handle and decide to change it after a period of time.

If you change your @handle, it doesn't mean you lose all of the Twitter followers who were following you on your previous @handle. You simply announce the change of @handle to your followers and your account remains intact in every other way.

Optimise your bio

The bio (biography) section (which is limited to 160 characters) allows you to showcase more about yourself or your organisation and it's probably one of the most important things people will check when they view your Twitter page. So optimising your bio is key. You can use keywords, signposts to URLs and even relevant #hashtags. However, first and foremost remember that you are writing your profile to appeal to people on Twitter rather than algorithms, so make sure your bio is human.

Tips for effective bio writing

1. Keep it simple. You only have 160 characters to complete your bio, so be succinct. Get your proposition across as clearly as possible.
2. You may want to show your personality by adding a personal titbit about yourself.
3. Steer clear of politics, religion or sexuality (unless your objective is to focus specifically on any of these elements).
4. Include relevant @handles and web URLs to signpost people to other platforms.
5. Include any relevant #hashtags – but only one or two.
6. Be sure that your bio is keyword optimised (but in an appealing way). For example, your bio would look pretty dull if it were just a string of keywords – and it would come across as a bit 'spammy' (e.g. 'Cat groomer – cat grooming – @ts – cat advice – cat expert'). It's better to turn those keywords into a 'human-friendly' sentence: 'Award-winning *cat groomer* and founder of *@happycats*, sharing *cat grooming* advice, tips and tactics on how to keep your *@ts* happy and stress-free.'

Clearly, the latter appeals, gets the proposition across – and also includes keywords, links and hashtags to better optimise your visibility on Twitter. (And it comes in at 146 characters, so it's well within the 160-character limit.)

A picture paints a thousand words

Your profile picture is one of the key elements people will review when deciding whether to follow you or engage with you. You should ensure that your profile picture fits with your objectives. Sticking with the cat groomer example, the profile picture could be of Mary Bloggs herself, perhaps holding a cat or an award; or it could be a picture of a beautifully groomed cat. A picture of Mary out with her friends in a bar probably wouldn't fit with her objectives. So, be sure your profile picture is fit for purpose.

Image sizes on Twitter

Your profile picture should be 128 x 128 pixels. It's a square. Therefore, you may need to consider how your brand fits into this space.

A new feature on Twitter allows you to include a Twitter 'header image'.

Your profile picture currently sits in the middle and your bio text is showcased below in white. If you don't include a header image, the background defaults to black (which is why the text is white). If you do include an image, you will need to consider how visible white text will be against your image.

To update the header image, simply click 'Edit profile' and select 'Design'.

(At the time of writing Twitter has only just introduced this feature and we suspect that by the time the book is published you will be able to a) change position of the profile pic and b) change the bio text to a different colour – but let's see.)

The suggested header image size is 1252 × 626 pixels, with a maximum file size of 5MB.

Should you post your tweets to Facebook? No!

When you are in 'edit profile' mode, at the foot of your profile you'll see an option to 'Post Tweets to your Facebook profile or Page'. Our advice is to steer well clear of this feature.

Think about it. Why would you waste valuable equity on your Facebook Page by simply sharing a 140-character tweet, which may contain Twitter terminology such as #hashtags or @handles.

Twitter is a completely different medium from Facebook. The time decay and frequency are significantly different on each: things stick around on Facebook Pages far longer than they do on Twitter; and you are likely to post things more frequently to Twitter than to your Facebook Page.

Our advice is to treat each channel separately. These shortcut buttons tend not to lead to engagement.

Who should you follow?

Once your profile page is complete and you're happy that it ticks all the boxes regarding your objectives, you are ready to get started on Twitter. However, let's remember **one critical thing: your objectives in using Twitter!**

Who you follow and what you talk about is determined by the objective of the account.

For example, we know of an accountancy firm that has three Twitter accounts. Each account has its own specific audience and objective.

- **Account 1** targets artists and gallery owners (a key client segment for the firm). The firm's objectives are to become thought leaders and 'go to' people about professional business and financial advice in this segment.
  - o *They follow:* artists and gallery owners and associated businesses, clients, influencers in the sector.
  - o *They talk about:* exhibitions, art, advice for the sector.
  - o *They share:* articles from their art blog, articles from influencers and about services and advice to the sector; Twitter updates from their other Twitter accounts; relevant retweets.
- **Account 2** targets restaurants and catering organisations (another key client segment for the firm).
  - o *They follow:* restaurants, catering organisations, influencers in the sector, relevant organisations, trade press, journalists, food writers.
  - o *They talk about:* foodie stuff, new restaurants, advice and topical news.
  - o *They share:* articles from their restaurant blog (they have three blogs, one to complement each Twitter account), topical news, advice to the sector; Twitter updates from their other Twitter accounts; relevant retweets.
- **Account 3** is their accountancy Twitter account, which targets new businesses and their clients.
  - o *They follow:* their clients, prospective clients, influencers in the sector, trade press, journalists, topical news, industry experts.
  - o *They talk about:* business, accounting news, tips, advice, topical news.
  - o *They share:* articles from their accountancy blog, topical news, advice, what the team are up to, updates in legislation, tax facts, etc.; Twitter updates from their other Twitter accounts; relevant retweets.

This shows that who they follow, what they talk about and what they share depends on the specific objective of each Twitter account. Having a separate account for each audience enables them to be highly targeted in their approach. However, where relevant, they can also share content and showcase their expertise and diversity.

Follow in a targeted way

Any marketer will agree that the more targeted a communication, the better the chance of success.

- Be sure to grow your following in a targeted way.
- Think about who is going to be influential for you.

Going back to the cat groomer example, think about who would be potential influencers for lead generation and thought leadership. A targeted list of who to follow might look like this:

- dog groomers (people might ask dog groomers if they do cat grooming – 'I don't, but I know an award-winning expert who does'
- cat trade press/journalists
- pet events/exhibitions
- cat owners
- people talking about cat grooming or looking for cat advice
- catteries ('Get your cat pampered while you're away')
- vets
- celebrities with cats.

We could go on. But what this illustrates is that you shouldn't start to follow just anyone; you should have a clear understanding of who may be influential and looking to engage with your product and services.

Remember, Twitter is a 'social' network, so when you are using the channel for business, it's fundamental that you utilise common-sense elements such as targeting. And the fact that Twitter is so 'real time' means that you can learn things very quickly.

While machine gun marketing – trying to hit as many people as possible – does often throw up some lucky hits, a targeted approach has always been a better way of using resources.

Learn about your network

As well as following in a targeted way, be sure to understand who the 'influential' people are in your network. Some will be noisier than others – they may be sharing your content more frequently, and they may be better connected.

It's important to keep growing your followers in a targeted way, but you should also focus on quality as well as quantity. The quality of people in your network is important. It's good to have a group of raving influencers who share your musings to a relevant audience every time you tweet. They are amplifying your reach and also advocating your conversations.

There's a great resource called www.twitcleaner.com, an app that enables you to see who is influential in your network and, indeed, those who are passive. It's a useful resource for keeping your Twitter network polished and effective.

Remember: Twitter won't allow you to open an account and then start following thousands of people all at once – you could be a spammer. Twitter has some clever algorithms at play that allow you to grow your following based on how many people follow you back. So you want to get the ratio right. If you're doing the relevant research, you should follow no more than 25–50 targeted followers a day. Twitter won't allow you to follow too many all at once. So take your time and grow that Twitter following in a targeted and authentic way.

Etiquette

We're often asked, 'If someone follows you, should you follow them back?' This is an interesting question because if you are doing all the right things and following people in a targeted way, if they then follow you, you've opened a conversation with a potential target.

If someone follows you, you're certainly not obliged to follow them back. You can check out their updates and see what they are tweeting about and then decide whether there's a fit. If you believe they could be useful or are well connected, then follow them.

As you know, there are ways they can be getting your attention if they are following you for a specific reason. So if you don't follow them back immediately, that's fine.

If you find that they are a perfect fit or a key influencer, you may want to send them a message back saying something along the lines of 'Great to connect. Look forward to talking in the future.' Or even one step further: 'I see you're also going to the XYZ event. Perhaps we should hook up?'

We do **not** advocate autoresponders being sent to every person that follows you (for example: 'Thanks for following. Why not check out our Facebook Page and get 20% off our cat food?') It's not targeted, it's pushy and it's really not very human. Imagine going into an offline networking scenario and adopting that approach. Quite!

A targeted starting point

Of course, once you understand who you want to follow, you can start looking for them. The search function on Twitter enables you to search by relevant keywords. Then you have the opportunity to review their Twitter stream, determine whether they have the right fit by seeing what they are talking about, then decide to follow them (or not). Twitter also has an advanced search option, which includes search operators that enable you to drill down even further.

You can also look at who they are following – or, indeed, who is following them. This is often a good way to go about finding new and relevant people to follow.

Finding the right people to follow can take a bit of time, but our advice is to put the effort in. Targeting your followers at the outset stands you in good stead for the future. After all, if you connect with key influencers and build a rapport they have the opportunity to retweet your content to their audiences, which in turn grows awareness into a targeted audience.

Tactical retweets

Whilst it's more effective to follow people in a targeted way, do remember that unless someone is following you back they can't actually see your tweets. A good tactic for getting people interested in you is to retweet their tweets. If they are saying something interesting, retweet their message (in effect this is a 'forward to all' function). Even if they aren't following you, and therefore can't see your tweets, they will be alerted to the fact that you have retweeted them. Every time someone mentions a Twitter @name or retweets a tweet, the person who is mentioned is notified. This may then compel them to check out who you are, and if you are of interest to them they may follow you.

And, of course, if you follow people they are following, they too may retweet what you are saying, and they'll be alerted to you that way too.

Direct @ messages

If you start a tweet directed to someone, for example: '@michellecarvill I really enjoyed your latest blog post. Thanks for sharing and keep them coming. Would be great to connect', the person you are addressing is alerted that someone has mentioned them. If you are using Twitter effectively, mentions are key as these can open conversations. (And you really should be tracking your mentions on Twitter.) Even though that person may not be following you, they will be alerted to your message and may feel compelled to check you out and follow you. This opens up the opportunity for them to share your tweets with their followers too.

Getting followed

Getting people to follow you is good news, particularly if they have a strong fit with your objectives. Once they follow you, your tweets are visible to them. And if they like what you are tweeting about and retweet what you have to say, all their followers will see your original tweet. (This is particularly good if they have thousands of followers. If, say, you've written a blog post and your follower retweets your link, it will very quickly be sent to thousands of people who may never have found your blog before.)

Another thing to do is register in the WeFollow directory (www.wefollow. com), using specific keywords so that you'll get picked up when people search on those keywords. It's also a good place to search for people.

Promote your Twitter @ handle

There are various places where you can promote the fact that people can follow you on Twitter, such as your email signature, your blog and your website. If you write articles and submit them to article marketing sites, your signature link can include your Twitter handle. Then there are your business card, letterhead, T-shirts, bags, point of sale materials, marketing campaigns, postcards, direct mail, appointment cards – depending on your objective, you can post it wherever relevant.

Replying to tweets

Once you're tweeting and seeing tweets appearing on your Twitter page from those you are following, you may want to reply to them. As discussed earlier, there are two ways to do this: a) publicly, by using the @handle or simply hitting the Reply link in the Twitter stream; or b) via direct message, either by using the direct message function or by putting a 'd' in front of their @handle, e.g. d @michellecarvill. Remember, you can send direct messages only to people you are following and who are following you.

What to tweet

As mentioned earlier in this chapter, our advice is to do quite a lot of listening and looking before you embark on actual tweeting. This will help you gain some insights into the type of content that resonates with your audience and you will be better equipped to start communicating.

The planning, listening and analysing process should have been put in place and you should have a clear, focused view on what you want to achieve before you actually engage.

Remember: You are what you tweet. Be careful what you advocate, as it reflects on you and your organisation.

Rather than simply sharing just one type of content – for example the latest post your blog, or replicating promotional offers – it's far better to create a mix of targeted content. Content ideas could be based on:

- an observation
- something you're reading
- what you're watching
- an event you are at or will be attending
- your own content (blog, newswire, landing page)
- someone else's content (another blog, video or article that resonates)
- having a chat with someone, posing a question, sharing an answer
- retweets – what someone else has tweeted. If relevant, add your own sentiment to their tweet.

What not to tweet

- **What you're having for lunch.** Who cares? Yes, a lot of people do tweet about what they're eating or about something completely inane which is totally off point and really isn't that compelling. Twitter does allow you to communicate your personality and humanise the business, but do keep in mind the whole point of this potentially far-reaching channel. By all means be casual, and be human. But don't bore people by sharing mundane nonsense. Remember the 'So what?' factor and avoid or minimise tweets that really don't add any value to the conversation. Ideally, keep your messaging 'on point'.
- **Anything you wouldn't say 'on the record'.** Our rule of thumb is that if you wouldn't say it to someone's face don't say it on Twitter. (And remember: even if you delete a tweet, it can still be archived on the internet and could still be found.)

Plan your content and approach

The diagram below highlights a number of facets that we've covered in this chapter. The matrix can help you map out the purpose of your Twitter account, who to follow, what content to create, how you will engage and what you will measure so that you can learn what's working.

There may be other elements that you need to build into your matrix. For example, if you're dealing with an international market you need to consider the times when you need to be visible.

A Strategic Approach to Using Twitter

Purpose	Follow	Create	Engage	Measure
Promote cat grooming event	Previous delegates Cat owners, Vets, Dog groomers etc.	Content relating to the event Interviews and speakers # for people to ask questions before event Videos of experts	Ask questions, share tips, advice Showcase what's on at the event	Number of interactions via the # Number of @ mentions Sign-ups
Lead generation	Target audience Influencers People talking about my products and services	Regular blog posts showcasing my knowledge Case studies, testimonial videos Ebook	Provide tips and advice Showcase expertise Encourage to download free ebook	Number of ebook downloads Data capture for marketing Number of @ mentions Site traffic

Resources could be another element to add to the matrix. Who is going to be responsible for the management of different accounts? You might need to break down activity on each account even further, particularly if you are running a specific promotional campaign.

Using the Twitter campaign planning template (see diagram below, you can apply practical objectives, specific outcomes, audience, tactics, offers and messaging, and elaborate on the metrics you are going to focus on.

Twitter campaign

Objective:

Desired outcome – KPI: (eg: 30 seats booked)

Target audience:

Tactics (the how):

Any offer?

Messaging:

Measurement:

Twitter is probably one of the most powerful viral marketing resources currently available, but campaigns are too often just thrown onto Twitter with no strategic or tactical thought. Remember the saying, 'Those who aim for nothing hit it with remarkable accuracy' and make sure you start with the end in mind and have your objectives covered.

Measure what matters

When it comes to measurement, you need to be sure that you are measuring what matters.

You may need to measure different things according to your objectives and organisational needs. For example, the team responsible for the brand are likely to be most concerned about metrics such as:

- positive mentions
- negative mentions
- the general sentiment of the audience.

The business development team are likely to have a different set of metrics that they're keen to measure.

- How many people completed the lead generation form?
- How much traffic did we generate?
- Data capture.
- Competition sign-ups.
- Followers and engagement.

There are a number of resources you can use to help you better understand engagement, such as:

- HootSuite (www.hootsuite.com), which features HootSuite Analytics
- TweetStats (www.tweetstats)
- TweetReach (www.tweetreach).

And, of course, good old Google Analytics. Google Analytics now includes a Social tab, so you can drill down into traffic and data specifically driven by social networks.

While you will need to determine your own metrics to measure, here are some typical areas of measurement to consider.

- **Reach.** Total number of followers. Effectively, this is your raw distribution power.
- **Response rate.** Average number of @replies per tweet. The number of people who responded to each link or question. (TweetReach is good for this data).
- **Branding and awareness.** How often people reference your company or products. (Useful tools such as Google Alerts or Social Mention enable you to track this.)

- **Tweet grade.** The overall effectiveness of your Twitter account. Calculates number of followers and their influence (www.tweetgrader.com is a useful tool from the generous Hubspot team).
- **Sales funnel.** The number of visitors from Twitter who visit your website/blog and convert into leads/customers. You can find this data using Google Analytics.

Twitter #hashtags: what they are and how to use them

However long a team or person has been using Twitter, it's clear that people are confused, and often fearful, of the relatively harmless but potentially powerful 'hashtag'. They often have questions such as 'Where do I get a hashtag from?', 'Who creates the hashtag for me?' and 'What if I use a hashtag that's already been created?'

As discussed at the start of this chapter, Twitter is a hugely versatile resource, and hashtags are a wonderful element of Twitter. In this Hashtag section, we'll cover:

- what a hashtag is
- how you go about creating them
- tips for leveraging them
- how to explore hashtags that are already out there

What is a hashtag?

We're all accustomed to the hash sign (#) on keyboards or phone keypads. On Twitter, the term 'hashtag' simply refers to when a # sign has been placed in front of a word or group of words (e.g. #superbowl, #glee, #londonriots, #havingabadday) to 'tag' or 'group' tweets that all mention the same hashtag.

> ### Example
>
> The popular satirical BBC news programme *Have I Got News for You* promotes the Hashtag #hignfy. People can share their opinions using the hashtag while the show is airing. If you go to the search box on Twitter and type in the hashtag #hignfy you can see the conversations that are happening or have happened around the programme.

With the growth in second and third screening (people using two or three screens at any one time, e.g. TV and laptop, tablet or smartphone), while you're watching the programme you can also watch the live buzz that's happening on Twitter. It's effectively a live conversation.

The people talking and sharing about #hignfy do not have to be following each other on Twitter, but they can all be discussing the programme, asking questions, sharing opinions, etc., simply by including the hashtag #hignfy in their tweets. If you wanted to find fans of the programme, you could search on #hignfy to see who is talking about it.

It's highly unlikely that any of the people talking about the programme would mention that they're fans in their Twitter profiles; so without hashtags we wouldn't know that they are fans or be able to reach and connect with that audience as easily.

A common thread

In effect, a hashtag is a way of searching for tweets that have a common topic. They are effectively an 'anchor' to group conversations that allows you to create communities of people all interested in the same topic. The hashtag makes it easier to find them and to share information related to a particular topic.

Example

For example, when the London riots kicked off in August 2011 anyone who wanted to know what was going on or to share what was happening could follow the news by searching #londonriots and share their news by including #londonriots in their tweets. The hashtag was used by thousands of people for different purposes. The police and emergency services used it to report updates, as did local authorities and the media; people searched on the hashtag to keep up to date with where there were problems and whether it was safe to get home. Remember, these people were in no other way connected – the only common factor was that they all wanted to know about or report on the London riots. Therefore, #londonriots became a topic that a diverse set of people were engaging with.

Similarly, when we deliver social media training, particularly through our training arm, Business Training Made Simple (www.businesstraining madesimple.co.uk), we share articles, tips, advice and offers via the hashtag #mymotraining while we are training. At the outset of any course, we advise delegates of the # and at the end of the course we go to Twitter search to show them the stream of information we have created during the course, and also show them tweets that already exist using the hashtag. This allows them to see all the resources and conversations happening around the hashtag. So it becomes a useful tool to share information and resources with a diverse audience. Previous course participants often check back to the #mymotraining hashtag because they know that we are always adding new things to it. Therefore it becomes a useful repository for up-to-date information about the subjects we cover in training.

Hashtags and trending on Twitter

If enough people talk about or mention the same hashtag it can 'trend'. (You can see 'trending topics' on the left-hand side of your Twitter home page.) 'Trending' simply means that there's a huge 'buzz' about a topic or hashtag; it's a topic that is 'being talked about the most' on Twitter.

If you click 'Change' you can set your trends to worldwide or country-specific, and you can often drill down further into a specific city.

During the summer of 2012 Twitter introduced a 'Get tailored Trends' feature. If you click this feature, it removes location factors and focuses on things that are trending that 'matter more to you'. How they work this out focuses on who you follow and what they are talking about.

Of course, trending on Twitter is no mean feat. With over 400 million tweets a day, your topic or hashtag really does have to get a lot of people talking about it to trend. So if it trends, that's quite an achievement.

Hashtags, search and awareness

As we've mentioned, searching for a #hashtag in Twitter Search is simple. Just go to Twitter Search and enter your # term to find out what's happening around a topic – or to see if a # exists.

When you're searching for a particular hashtag, you may find other ones too – variations on a theme – so it may be worth investigating those other associated hashtags to see what conversation is happening around them.

And don't just search Twitter – search Google too. Hashtags make their way across into traditional searches, as does other content from the social platforms.

Promoting a hashtag

As outlined in the Nike example earlier in the chapter, Nike showcased a whole campaign around the hashtag #makeitcount. This is a growing advertising tactic, with TV programmes using hashtags throughout the airing. We saw in Chapter 1 that the TV programme *Bank of Dave* aired the hashtag #bankofdave approximately 12 times throughout the hour the programme was broadcast.

The # promotion is a very interesting facet of advertising and one that seems to be becoming increasingly popular. After all, it gives brands and advertisers a mechanism to anchor a community of diverse people around an online conversation by widely promoting the #. And if your audience is on Twitter, it's a great way to get people participating in your advertising campaign.

Where you do get hashtags?

Anyone can create a hashtag. There isn't a repository where you go and 'get one'. You can simply create one yourself by adding the simple # before typing a keyword or group of words. However, it's a good idea to check out a hashtag before you start promoting it. You need to be sure the hashtag you are planning to use is unique and isn't already associated with something totally irrelevant.

Example

Let's say you're running an event for veterinary surgeons. You've got 300 people coming, and so there's no way you're going to be able to have a one-to-one conversation with each of those delegates. You may be able to take a few questions from the floor, but that won't give you the opportunity to engage with every delegate who may have a question. By promoting a hashtag for your event and showcasing this at the outset in your promotional materials you can get people connecting and talking – before, during and after the event. Let's say you want to create a brand or hashtag for the event, such as #vetsandpets. You would go to Twitter, search for that hashtag and see if it is being used elsewhere.

Remember, tweets are limited to 140 characters, so you don't want to use a ridiculously long hashtag, e.g. #vetsandpetsannualevent2013. Keep it short and simple – #vetsandpets.

Tapping into relevant audiences via hashtags

To promote your event to a wider targeted audience, you may want to check out other hashtags to see if you can tap into other audiences using hashtags that are appropriate and relevant to your forthcoming event.

For example, you might start by checking out #vets to see what that pulls in. We did this and found a lot of tweets about 'veterans' – but when we searched #veterinary, we found a number of related hashtags. These would be worth exploring and perhaps using in tweets alongside the #vetsandpets event hashtag to grow even more awareness into a targeted audience.

However, a word of warning here – **you should not** hijack for promotional purposes totally unrelated trending or popular hashtags. The term 'mashtagging' is defined in the *Urban Dictionary* as:

> **Mashtag**
>
> *n.* A social networking status update, tweet, or post that contains an unnecessarily large number of tags or tagged names often unrelated to the context of the post.

There have been a few incidents where brands have piggy-backed on trending topics, often highly sensitive topics, such as #Cairo and #Egypt around the time of the 2011 uprising, in a totally unrelated way and they came off really badly.

In late 2009 Habitat UK's tweets included well-known brand hashtags or trending hashtags to promote their products to a wider audience.

Since when did HabitatUK sell Apple products? The onslaught that followed their hijacking attempts was not pretty.

And as if that wasn't enough, Twitter can close your account if they think you're out to spam by using hashtags incorrectly. So beware. If enough people complain or report you to Twitter, it could be goodbye to your Twitter account.

Hashtags: key points

- Check whether the hashtag you want to promote is already in use. A simple search on Twitter should do it.
- Look for other relevant hashtags and review who is talking around the topic – they may be relevant for you to talk to too.
- **Never** jump onto trending or popular hashtags that are totally irrelevant to your promotion or conversation. It's spam, it's frowned upon and those who have done it have found that their reputation has been badly damaged.
- If you want other relevant audiences to find your conversations, use a keyword-enabled hashtag that they can search on.
- If you're using a bespoke hashtag for an event or campaign, be sure to promote the hashtag so that users know about it.

Twitter lists and segmenting the people you follow

Twitter lists are just what they say – lists of Twitter accounts. Used effectively, they're a great way to organise who you are following (and even who you are not following) into groups categorised by you. You can use your lists to tidy up your feed and group together tweeters and their tweet streams. Lists allow you to view tweets in separate feeds and follow targeted, categorised groups of people together.

For example, if you were researching 'cat groomers' on Twitter and wanted to follow a selection of people who are tweeting and talking about cat grooming you could find all the cat groomers on Twitter and then group them into a list. (Note: you don't have to follow them to put them into your list.) Having them all in one list will allow you to look only at tweets that are about cat grooming, which allows you to focus your attention and cut through the noise being made by the various other people you follow on your Twitter stream.

In a separate list you might like to group all your old college or university friends – that way you can simply click on their list and view all their streamed tweets together. This works especially well if you like to tweet each other a lot – you can block out all other Twitter noise and focus on the conversation going on between the people in your college list.

Another use for a Twitter list is to group all employees together. Having an employee list means that you can see the conversations the people within your business are having.

Finding new and relevant people

Lists also help you to target and find new and useful contacts. For example, when you view your lists you can see lists that you have created as well as lists of which you are a member (list that someone else may have put you into).

Let's say you've been put into a 'UK Bloggers' list. Someone has gone to the trouble of creating a list of UK bloggers. People in that list may also be useful for you, so you can access that list and review and see who you would like to follow.

How to create a Twitter list

Creating a list is very simple.

1. Log in to your Twitter account.
2. Go to the List section by clicking the cog on the upper right-hand side of the top bar.

3. Click Lists. Now you can view your lists and the lists that others have put you into. You can also create a list.
4. To create a list click 'Create list' and then choose a name for your list.
5. Decide whether you want your list to be public or private (only you can view a private list).
6. Click 'Create list'. And that's it.

7. Now you can add users and search for people to add to your list – you can do this from your profile page or from any following page. To add a person to a list simply click on the person icon next to the Follow/Following button and select 'Add or remove from lists'.

Private and open lists

When you create a list you can decide whether your list will be open or private. If it's open anyone can see that list. If it's private, only you see it. This is a great way to monitor your competitors, or anyone else you would rather they didn't know that you were following them.

Are there any limitations to lists?

As far as we can see, the rules that applied when lists came out in 2009 still apply. Lists can grow to no more than 500 people and each account can have a maximum of 20 lists. So there's plenty of scope there.

Do I want to be on other people's list?

The simple answer to this question is yes, you do. Being in other people's lists means that you will become more visible to your target audience. For example, if you are a cat groomer you want to be picked up by someone who's making lists about cat groomers. You are more likely to get followed by people looking for cat groomers and it's verification that you've been tagged by others as a 'cat groomer' too.

Twitter is a content-rich channel and lists help you to sift through the noise and listen to targeted tweeters who are talking about what you want to hear. If you're on someone's list you are far more likely to be found by the right kind of tweeter.

Can you target tweets directly to Lists?

At the time of writing (about six months before publication – which is why we're running a blog alongside the book to manage all the updates and changes) you cannot currently direct conversations to a list segment.

Given that you can segment those you follow so that you can see what a particular segment of people are talking about, it shouldn't be too difficult for the team at Twitter to find a way of enabling you to tweet into a segment. This may be a paid-for service in the future and possibly one of the ways Twitter will look to monetise their site – who knows. But given that the functionality works one way, it would certainly make an attractive proposition to be able to target conversations into segments. Let's wait and see.

Useful Twitter apps

- Tweetgrader.com (http://tweet.grader.com) from the @hubspot team – grades your account.
- TwitCleaner (www.twitcleaner.com) – tidy Twitter/influencers.
- Twilert (www.twilert.com) – set specific alerts. Similar to Google Alerts, but for Twitter.
- Tweetreach (http://tweetreach.com) – useful research analysis tool.
- Who.Unfollowed.Me (http://who.unfollowed.me) – see who unfollowed you.
- Buffer (www.bufferapp.com) – bookmark for tweets and optimised schedule.
- Tweetdeck (www.tweetdeck.com) – scheduler.
- Twtpoll (www.twtpoll.com) – polls/surveys.
- Twellow (www.twellow.com) – categorised search directory.

There are literally hundreds, probably thousands, of apps and resources to help Twitter be an even more wonderful place. Those listed above are just a few of the ones we've used over the years.

Social media marketing action plan

- Think strategically – Plan, Listen and Analyse before you Engage.
- Know what your Twitter account is about and plan your content and conversation accordingly.
- Revisit your business objectives – use Twitter smartly to achieve objectives.
- Think about how you are going to blend Twitter into your marketing activities to add value and leverage.
- Get your service recovery process/escalation procedures, terms and conditions, and disclaimers in place. (See the social media guidelines in Chapter 11.)
- Use hashtags wisely.
- Leverage Twitter lists to manage your followers.
- Follow in a targeted and purposeful way.
- Remember, measurement and analysis aids continuous learning.

5 | Facebook: the 'new newspaper'

What you will learn from this chapter:

- How businesses can use Facebook
- Differences between a Facebook profile and a Facebook Page
- What to post on your Facebook Page
- Increasing customer engagement with your Page
- Community management
- Facebook advertising

In the nine years that Facebook has been around, it has evolved from a simple way for college students to chat to each other into a truly global phenomenon. There are now 1 billion users of this social networking site – a staggering one in seven of the world's population.

For thousands of people around the world, the first engagement they have with the outside world when they wake up in the morning is not TV, radio or a newspaper. Instead, it is very likely to be their Facebook news feed on their mobile or tablet device. Facebook is aware of this and its game plan is to take on the internet itself. Instead of going online and surfing sites using browsers such as Explorer, Firefox or Safari, you would stay within Facebook and have all your favourite sites come to you via your news feed. In effect, your personal news feed has become your own, tailored online newspaper.

To explain further, let's look at how a traditional newspaper is put together. Typically the news editor will start off with sheets of blank paper. First to go in will be the advertisements, then off-the-shelf feature stories and finally the news. This will have come from a variety of sources including journalists, other media outlets, PR agencies and so on.

Ultimately, though, it is the news editor (perhaps the editor or maybe even the proprietor) who decides what the paper's target audience will want to read, based on the demographic of the readership. So the news editor of a tabloid-style newspaper like the *Star* will have a mixture of sport, celebrity gossip, national news and showbiz while over at the *Financial Times* the content will be more cerebral – market trends, national and international business news, informed comment, etc.

However, by the very nature of newspapers, the content is quite generic and will not all be of interest to readers. In fact, how many times have you ever read your chosen newspaper cover to cover? This is unlikely to happen, as you choose to read only what is of specific interest to you.

To summarise, a newspaper is a collection of advertisements and editorial which is published either daily, weekly or monthly; news is gathered from a variety of sources and content is decided by a news editor.

facebook : the new newspaper!

The news feed in Facebook, whether within a user's personal profile or a brand's Page, is very similar. When a new account is set up or a new Page created, you start off with a blank canvas. Over time, this will be filled with a combination of news, features and adverts (more on this later).

As with a newspaper, there is a variety of news sources:

- friends
- groups
- Pages
- subscriptions
- Facebook ads
- apps
- offers
- check ins, and of course . . .
- **you** as the owner of the profile or the Page.

You are also now likely to see a variety of adverts as sponsored stories or promoted/targeted posts, as well as offers and competitions – more on which later.

However, unlike with newspapers, you are in effect the editor, news editor and reporter for your news 'feed', and thereby you get to choose what you want to see.

With hundreds of millions of people getting their daily information from their personalised news feeds, it is not hard to understand why Facebook has become such a powerful force. And inevitably, even newspapers now market themselves on Facebook in an attempt to get their brand across via this new medium. Check out www.facebook.com/guardiantechnology, www.facebook.com/latimes or www.facebook.com/lemonde.fr to see how papers are using the site.

As with newspapers, though, you have a responsibility not only to provide interesting and engaging content but also to be very careful about not publishing anything that could be harmful, libellous or offensive.

Ways of using Facebook

Throughout this book we emphasise the importance of using social networks to meet specific business objectives, and Facebook is no different. The site can be used for a wide range of different purposes, so it is vital that you plan how you are going to use it for your particular organisation.

It may be that Facebook can be used in a number of different ways, so you may even consider having different Pages to reflect this.

These are the key ways we think Facebook can be used by businesses.

- **Customer support and service:** communicate directly with your customers.
- **Lead generation:** drive traffic to your website or Page using organic and paid for marketing.
- **Polling and product feedback mechanism:** Facebook has this built into Pages.
- **Corporate and social responsibility channel:** reveal a different, less corporate side of your brand.
- **News distribution:** can be a great way to inform your client base about important news.
- **Brand awareness and establishment:** get people talking about your products or brands.
- **Product and event promotion:** reach out to your target audiences and engage with potential customers.
- **Gathering support for a cause:** a fantastic way for charities to educate and inform people.
- **Humanising your brand:** showcase the people who work within your organisation.
- **Research:** use Facebook Insights to learn about consumer behaviour.
- **Competitions:** target your customer base with interesting and content-rich competitions.
- **Check-in deals:** reward customer loyalty.

Personal Facebook profiles and Facebook Pages

We have been using the terms 'profile' and 'Page'. There are very important distinctions to be made between the two and many individuals and companies get the two mixed up.

In essence, there are three ways in which you can have a presence on Facebook: a profile; a group; and a Page.

Facebook profiles

A profile belongs to an individual and is their personal account. Typically, this is the place where you share information with your family and friends. A profile can be used to set up a group or manage a Page. Ideally, it should be kept personal and not be used for business purposes.

Note: many brands/organisations set up a profile for their business, when they should have created a Page. If you use a personal profile for business, you are essentially a brand or organisation masquerading as a real person. This is not condoned by Facebook. Facebook terms and conditions state that you aren't supposed to 'use your personal profile for commercial gain'.

Subscribe feature

However, let's say that, as the owner of an organisation, you're the 'voice' behind the brand. Perhaps people want to talk directly to you and find out what your organisation is doing, via you rather than via a corporate Facebook Page. Facebook profiles can be 'subscribed' to, which means that users can 'subscribe' to your profile to get your news on their personal profile news feeds.

Therefore, if you are talking about what you are doing in your business, rather than using your profile for profit, that's quite different.

> ### Example
>
> Take a look at Arianna Huffington's personal profile: www.facebook.com/AriannaHuffington.
>
> There is also a great article from @smexaminer that's well worth reading: www.socialmediaexaminer.com/promote-your-business-with-facebook/#more-19427.

Facebook groups

A group is a community of people and friends who promote, share and discuss relevant topics – similar to an online forum. It can be closed (anyone can see members but not posts), open (anyone can see members and posts) or secret (both members and posts are hidden to non-members). Although a group is a useful way for people, fans or friends to communicate, it should not be confused with a Page. Individuals can administer the group from their personal profile.

Facebook Pages

A Page is a business or organisation's branded presence on Facebook. It can act either as an ancillary presence to a company website or, increasingly for consumer-facing brands, it can even replace the website, becoming the centre of an organisation's online marketing strategy. Pages can be branded too: just in the same way you secure a www address for your website, you can register your brand or organisation name, e.g. www.facebook.com/mybrand. Pages can be administered via a personal profile.

For more information on the difference between groups and Pages on Facebook, check out this excellent blog: www.facebook.com/blog/blog.php?post=324706977130.

In order to be the administrator of a Page, it is advisable to have some form of personal profile on Facebook. While it is possible to create a Page without a profile, you have much less flexibility and you cannot administer multiple Pages, as you can via a live personal profile.

Facebook policies and procedures

As with Twitter, you should Plan, Listen and Analyse before deciding to Engage. It is important to do the correct preparation in advance of setting up a Facebook Page. You also need to have a sensible policy in place for your staff about what they can and cannot do on the site.

We would suggest that every member of staff who has a Facebook account should set their privacy settings to maximum – i.e. only their friends can see their posts.

Also, as extra protection, all staff should ensure that their profile picture is not in any way harmful to their professional standing. Even with your privacy settings set to maximum, if you are on Facebook, your profile can be found. Even though non-friends will not be able to look at your profile, your picture will be visible, so make sure it is suitable.

Whether we like it or not, many employers, prospective employers and potential customers now go straight to Facebook (as well as LinkedIn)

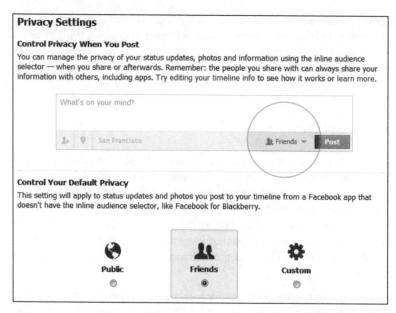

to find out more about the person they are going to be dealing with. If your privacy settings are set to 'public' or you have an unsuitable profile picture, they may find out more than you had bargained for!

Moving into a slightly greyer area, it may be worth providing your staff with guidelines about what they should *maybe think about* when using their personal profiles. Clearly, you do not control what your staff do in their private lives, but there could be times when what they post will harm your organisation.

> ### Example
>
> Julie, one of your junior members of staff, makes a racist remark on her Facebook profile. Although her profile is visible only to her friends, one of Julie's friends decides to share the comment, not only with his friends, but he also makes the comment public.

We would advise setting up some simple guidelines for staff, which are just as much about protecting themselves as about ensuring your brand is not damaged.

- Don't write anything overtly offensive.
- Don't post anything that you wouldn't say to someone at work face-to-face – colleagues or managers alike.
- Be careful when voicing political, religious or potentially extremist opinions.
- Beware of libel – it is a criminal offence on Facebook, as with any other form of the written word, to publish anything false that could be damaging to a person's reputation.

- Watch out for photos you may post or photos you are tagged in – nudity and drunkenness rarely look good!
- Think about your profile. It is essentially the online personification of who you are.

Setting up and managing a Page

If you decide to set up a Facebook Page you have two key options.

1. If you don't have a Facebook account or if the administrators in your company or organisation are likely to change rapidly, go to www. facebook.com/pages and create a Page following the instructions on screen. It would be advisable to set up an email account (e.g. facebook@mycompany.co.uk) to log in to this account. When you need to administer the Page, go to www.facebook.com and log in to the account.
2. If you have a profile, then you already have a Facebook account. So if you are going to be the Page 'owner', simply log in to your profile, then go to www.facebook.com/pages, where you'll see a Create Page button. Click on this and you will be taken through to this page:

Local Business or Place

Company, Organization or Institution

Brand or Product

Artist, Band or Public Figure

Entertainment

Cause or Community

You'll see that there are six categories to choose from. Select the one most appropriate to your business or organisation, check the box saying you agree with Facebook's terms of business (www.facebook.com/page_guidelines.php) and away you go.

Note: if you have a business which is defined by its geographical area – a butcher's shop in Tunbridge Wells or a hairdresser in Hamburg – it is be best to choose the Local Business or Place option. The reason for this is that you can geo-locate (promote your location), allowing your customers to 'check in' via Facebook on their mobile devices when they come to your premises.

Don't worry if you are unsure about how to categorise your Page – you can always change the category later using the admin settings (www. facebook.com/help/?faq=222732947737668).

When you want to administer the Page from a personal profile, go to your personal account and in the top right-hand corner of the screen you'll see an arrow to the right of the Home button. Click on this arrow

icon and a drop-down menu will appear:

Once you click on any of the Pages that you manage, you will be leaving your personal profile and logging in to the Page (in much the same way as you would log in to the content management system of a website).

Note: once you've logged in to the Page, there is no reference at all to you being an administrator of that Page. No one will see anything related to your personal profile at all. Switching from a personal profile to a Page administrator is completely anonymous to everyone else.

However you wish to manage your Page, there are several steps you will need to take before you officially 'publish' it.

Step 1

Ensure that you have the right number of administrators and you have allocated them specific roles. As the creator of the Page, you may want to have one or more other appointed people to help manage it. They can have differing levels of control over the Page. Administrators must have a Facebook account, they need to have Liked your Page and they should provide you with the email address they use to access the site. You can manage administrators at any time by clicking the Admin Roles tab in the admin panel:

When you are making people administrators, you can allocate them to any of five different levels of access to the Page, from simply viewing the Insights (more on Insights later), right up to full control. See the diagram below for more details:

	Manager	Content Creator	Moderator	Advertiser	Insights Analyst
Manage Admin Roles	✓				
Edit the Page and Add Apps	✓	✓			
Create Posts as the Page	✓	✓			
Respond to and Delete Comments	✓	✓	✓		
Send Messages as the Page	✓	✓	✓		
Create Ads	✓	✓	✓	✓	
View Insights	✓	✓	✓	✓	✓

Step 2

Go to www.facebook.com/username and register the name of the Page. You can choose either something brand-specific (e.g. www.facebook.com/SimonHowieButchers) or that is keyword-enabled (e.g. www.facebook.com/HotelsinLondon).

Step 3

Make sure you have a decent 'cover' image for your Page. This should be 850 x 315 pixels in size and, like the cover of a book or old-fashioned LP record, must entice people onto your Page.

In creating your cover photo image, Facebook advises that you:

- **use a unique image that represents your Page.** This might be a photo of a popular menu item, album artwork or a picture of people using your product.

- **be creative and experiment** with images your audience responds well to.
- **use the cover photo to bring a strong visual impact to your Page** by extending your brand with lifestyle imagery, product images or a description of your services.

Facebook has strict guidelines about the cover photo, see www.facebook.com/page_guidelines.php for full details. We strongly advise you to **adhere to these guidelines**. Facebook doesn't overtly state what it will do to police this policy or what it will do if your cover photo doesn't follow the rules, but once you've put time and effort into creating a Page you probably don't want to take the risk of finding out!

Step 4

Your company or organisation logo must fit the 180 × 180 pixel square. If it doesn't, you may need to get your logo redesigned so it can fit the space.

Step 5

In the 'About' section of the Page, you need to put a succinct and, ideally, keyword-enabled 'boilerplate' which sums up the purpose of your business or organisation, your mission statement and an overview of what you do, complete with appropriate websites.

See the Dove Page, www.facebook.com/dove/info, for a good example of this.

At the same time, it is a good idea to list the terms and conditions for your Page. This is especially important if it is being used as a customer service/engagement channel. A great example can be found on the British Airways Facebook Page, www.facebook.com/britishairways/app_244263645687417. It has actually turned this into an app (called House Rules) on its Page.

Step 6

Build up your 'timeline' from the date your organisation was founded up to the present time. To do this, upload as many relevant photos and videos as you can, along with write-ups. This will provide a background narrative as well as help reinforce your brand for visitors to the Page. Remember, you want your Facebook Page to look just as engaging as your website – if not more so – therefore invest time making it look the best you can.

Note: The first 'milestone' you add to your Facebook Page should be the 'oldest', i.e. when your organisation was launched or founded.

Step 7

Think about what applications (apps) you could have for your Page. You can see four tabs when you first visit the Page, including Photos (a default app that you can't move or remove). You can add another eight. In effect, these tabs act as 'sub pages' and can be anything from online adverts to games and even e-commerce facilities.

It is also possible to move these apps around so that your four most important ones are immediately visible on your Facebook Page. To move them, click on the Edit icon on the top right-hand corner and select the tabs you want to move around. Check out www.facebook. com/joinparkbench to see how a Page can be configured.

Step 8

Decide whether you want fans of your Page to be able to message you. In the Admin settings, you can check or uncheck a box under Messages:

If you decide to check this, anyone who Likes your Page will see this on the right-hand side of your Page:

They will then be able to send you through a private message.

Note: You cannot initiate conversations with your fans. They must contact you first.

Customising your Page

Every Facebook Page is built on exactly the same platform, so whether you have a small bakery in Melton Mowbray or you are Coca Cola, exactly the same criteria apply. However, you can customise your Page using apps, templates and menu settings.

You can download and manage off-the-shelf Facebook Page packages from websites such as www.wix.com or www.pagemodo.com, or you could contact local web designers and/or online creative agencies who can build you bespoke applications and templates.

Engagement tactics

You have your Page set up, you've filled your timeline with engaging content, you've added applications and you've made sure the right people are going to administer the site. You're now ready to publish the Page. This is easily be done. You will see a link which says 'Publish Your Page' at the top of the screen (more here: www.facebook.com/help/?faq+=184605634921611).

Once you have clicked this link, the Page will be visible to anyone who isn't an administrator and this will herald the end of the first phase of creating a Facebook Page.

The next phase involves publicising the Page and getting people to hit the all-important Like button. This button is situated underneath the cover photo on the right-hand side and it's one step in getting people to engage with the Page. Clicking Like is akin to subscribing to a blog or opting in to an email newsletter.

Note: Many brands think that all they have to do is get customers/fans/clients to Like the Page. They then measure how successful it is by the number of Likes. However, Liking is just the *start* of a journey which involves getting those people to interact and engage with the Page.

During our training courses, we are often asked how to get people to start Liking Pages. There is no simple answer. It is about creating a defined strategy using an array of different techniques, a few of which are listed here.

- **Print the Page's URL** on traditional marketing materials such as advertisements, business cards, flyers and posters.
- **Put the Facebook Like button** on your website in all the appropriate pages.
- **Word of mouth:** tell your customers about your Page.
- **Point of sale promotion:** we were in a music shop the other day and on the counter was a business card that promoted only its Facebook Page: 'Follow us on Facebook to join the conversation and get exclusive events and discounts.' Simple!
- **Point of sale interaction:** if a customer has had a good experience or they make a comment about loving the products you sell, ask them if they have a Facebook account. If they have, offer them a good reason to Like the Page, e.g. 'If you liked the stay in our hotel/meal in our restaurant/our shoes, Like our Facebook Page and we will have lots of special offers/interesting news/fashion tips.'

- **Competitions:** just as in traditional marketing, these are a great way of engaging with potential customers. Again, use either traditional marketing materials or online marketing such as email campaigns and websites to entice people to your Page. However, it is important that you read Facebook's promotional guidelines before setting up your competition (www.facebook.com/page_guidelines.php). If you don't, your Page can be disabled by Facebook.
- **Advertising:** this is now a highly cost-effective and targeted way of increasing the Likes to your Page or driving traffic to your website. There are a variety of methods of doing this – more later on in this chapter.
- **Partnerships:** as with other forms of affiliate marketing, these can be a great way to advertise your Pages. By partnering with complementary brands that have a highly visible Facebook presence, you can gain more exposure for your product or service.
- **Networking:** no company or organisation works in isolation and the same is true on Facebook. Speak to other businesses in your area and look at Liking each other's Pages. For example, a hotel could Like the Facebook Pages for local restaurants, cab companies, leisure attractions, shops and bars.
- **Offers:** owners of Pages have the opportunity to promote offers in-store and/or online in the same way as Groupon or Vouchercodes. More information can be found at www.facebook.com/help/pages/offers.

EdgeRank: the visibility score used by Facebook

A far better measure of how well the Page is performing is the 'talking about this' figure, which shows how many people have actually had some form of interaction with the Page over the previous week.

> **Example: Ford UK**
>
> Just over 4% of the people who Like this Page have interacted with it. Overall, only a tiny percentage of people who Like a Page ever go back and visit it again (http://bit.ly/JrecYt).

The vast majority of people and organisations who use Facebook have never heard of EdgeRank, a mathematical algorithm that automatically measures how visible profiles and Pages are on the site.

As so much information is being posted every day by people and organisations all round the world, Facebook has had to institute a policy of filtering what information can be seen in news feeds. If it didn't, the site would go into overload!

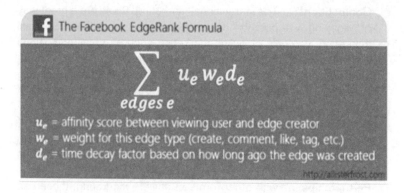

Three key ingredients go into making up a score on EdgeRank.

1) **Affinity.** This is based on the proximity to or how 'friendly' you are with a person or a brand on Facebook. It measures interactions – Likes, Comments, Clicks, Shares or Wall Posts – that users have with your profile or Page. Put simply, this means that you need to engage with the fans of your Page by posting content that will be shared in some way.

2) **Edge Weight.** This variable decides which pieces of content are more likely than others to appear in news feeds. A strong emphasis is put on photos, videos and links rather than plain, text-only updates. So this is all about posting interesting, engaging content.

3) **Recency.** Put simply, newer content is more likely to appear than older content. The message here is to post regularly!

Note: You don't see your EdgeRank score. The only way you can monitor how well your Page is faring on Facebook is to look at your Insights – these will measure how people have been interacting with the content you post.

The key thing is not to get hung up about your EdgeRank score, and to make sure your Page ranks as highly as possible. And we have six easy tips.

Tip 1

Post plenty of photos and videos. Just as with newspapers, it is far more interesting when stories are illustrated with photos or diagrams.

Tip 2

Don't be afraid to ask your fans for their opinions. Many brands make the mistake of simply 'pumping' out information on their Facebook

Pages, just as they have in the past with adverts or traditional market-ing. However, social media is very different and should always be treated as a community or one-to-one conversation. Facebook Pages should act like a forum where people with shared interests can have conversa-tions. And, like any conversation, rather than a monologue, you want to hear the opinions of others. So, rather than post something about what you or your brand are doing, simply ask a question. It could be related to what you do or something topical.

Tip 3

Use the polling function to invite comment. Even better than asking a question, you can carry out a free poll using your Page. When you click on the Event, Milestone + button you get a drop-down menu which includes Question. Click on this and you'll then be given the opportunity to add polling options:

Click on this and you can then add polling options:

Tip 4

Don't post too little or too often – find your pace. Until recently, it was accepted practice that you should post no more than once a day on Facebook Pages. However, with the advent of Timeline, the more quality content you can post, the better. In fact, many successful brands are now posting hourly or more. Clearly, many companies or organisations will not have the resources to post this much, but it is important to try to update your Page at least once a day. Pages that are updated only weekly or less will not only rank lower on EdgeRank but will also not look great from an engagement perspective.

During your planning phase, you need to factor in the time required to keep the Page regularly updated. There is now the option to schedule your posts in advance using the new Page Scheduler. So if you don't want to post in the evening or weekends, there is still a way of updating your Page with content. To do so, simply update your status as usual, then specify when you would like it to be published – exactly as you would with Twitter or LinkedIn on a social media dashboard such as Hootsuite.

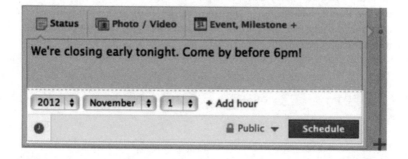

Note: It is important to bear in mind the times when your audience are most likely to be engaged with your Page.

You can also use Scheduler to backdate posts. Say, for example, you have been at an event and haven't had time to post on your timeline. You can retrospectively add in these posts to within a 15-minute time slot. Check out this great blog which looks at scheduling in more detail: www.socialmediaexaminer.com/facebook-scheduled-posts.

Tip 5

Use the correct tone of voice for your brand. It is important that you think about the language you use and the tone of voice you employ when engaging with your Facebook community of customers or fans. As with other forms of marketing, think about your audience. Depending on what business objective(s) you want to achieve with your Page – driving traffic to your website, building your brand, customer service etc. – the audience may differ significantly. Using corporate language may be fine on a website but may not work on a Page, especially if it is being used for corporate and social responsibility purposes.

And if you are using the Page as a customer services channel, you may wish to employ a tone of voice similar to what you would use in a call centre or face-to-face setting.

Tip 6

Track the performance of your posts using Insights. Using Facebook Insights gives you access to a wealth of data, comparable to that provided by Google Analytics (www.google.com/analytics). This can be measured over specified time periods and exported as a CSV or Excel spreadsheet. It can also be broken down into a defined geographical spread and demographic profile.

Note: You need to have at least 30 fans of your Page to get access to Insights data.

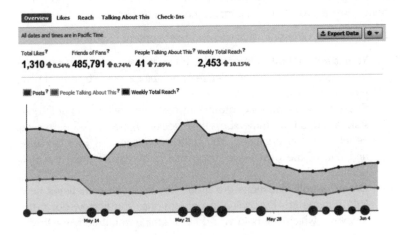

Facebook Insights will give you the following information.

- **Overview** gives you information on how many people have interacted with your individual posts and how the Page is performing overall.
- **Likes** lets you know where and who the people who Like your Page are. It also informs you how they came to Like the Page.
- **Reach** illustrates how many people you have reached through organic, paid or viral means.
- **Talking about this** informs you how many people have interacted with your Page in a seven-day period.
- **Check in** denotes the number of people who have checked in to your geographical location from a computer or mobile device in the previous seven days.

With this data, you will quickly learn more about your audience and the sort of information they get excited about. Therefore, if you are posting information which you believe to be engaging and no one is commenting on it, the chances are you need to change your engagement strategy or the quality of your updates.

In conjunction with Google Analytics, Facebook Insights will give you the opportunity to hone your marketing strategy and make the necessary changes to ensure that you are achieving your objectives or hitting pre-defined key performance indicators.

What to post on your Page

Using our newspaper analogy, your Facebook Page should be filled with content that educates, informs and entices your fan base. Ideally, you need a good selection of posts, images, videos, links, polls and questions – just as you would in a magazine or a newspaper.

Here are eight different ways you can post content to your Page.

1. **Your own content:** this could be content from your blog or news feed, a version of a press release or an opinion piece by one of your members of staff.
2. **Share someone else's content:** including content from other Pages.
3. **Ask a question:** remember that social media is about having continuous conversations. You want to engage with your fan base and one of the best ways to do this is by asking them for their opinions.
4. **Create a poll:** questions are great, but they can sometimes be a little untargeted. By adding in poll options, you narrow down the answers, which will help you do something constructive with the data.
5. **Observations:** pass comment on subjects that could be of interest to your fans.
6. **Recommendations:** showcase recommendations you have been given or publicly praise members of your own team.
7. **Talk about another Page:** mention a partner organisation's Page or post about a really engaging Page that may be of interest to your fan base. You can also put the @ symbol in front of the Page to highlight it.
8. **Respond to comments:** Facebook is about conversations. Some of them you will start; others will be started by your fans. Make sure you engage with them.

At the same time, we have a few pointers for what you shouldn't be posting on Facebook.

1. Updates that may be defamatory or inflammatory.
2. Anything that will not help you to meet your objectives for your Facebook Page.
3. Badly put together content such as blurry images, misspelt posts and incorrect links.
4. Anything you wouldn't say publicly.
5. Tweets. Keep them on Twitter!

Posts on Facebook

There are two ways you can post. You can create an update (maximum length 420 characters) or you can post a note which is essentially a longer version of an update (unlimited characters) with a headline.

Updates should be short and snappy ways of announcing something, drawing attention to a link or captioning a photograph. You don't have a headline, so try to make what you are writing stand out. Also remember to use a couple of your keywords. It is also possible to 'pin' your updates to the top of your Timeline. Go to the appropriate post, click on the Edit tab and pin it. The post will then stay at the top of your timeline for seven days. It is a little like creating a landing page on a website.

Notes are more akin to blogs, which you can also tag. To access notes, go to your Page and look for the Notes tab on the left-hand side under Apps. Think of each note as a miniature blog. It makes sense to use the normal blogging guidelines – short paragraphs, good use of keywords, simple language and no more than 400 words if possible.

Images on Facebook

Earlier on in the chapter, we talked about the importance of images on Facebook and how they need to meet specific criteria. Here is a handy table (thanks to www.jonloomer.com) which shows the dimensions required for maximum usability.

- Cover: 851 × 315 pixels
- Profile: 180 × 180 pixels
- Custom tabs: 111 × 74 pixels
- Shared photo: 403 × 403 pixels
- Highlighted photo: 843 × 403 pixels (you can highlight photos in your timeline to make them appear much bigger)
- Milestone: 843 × 403 pixels

We recommend that you get used to sizing your photos using free software such as www.irfanview.com or www.picresize.com so that they display properly on your timeline.

Note: As with anything online, make sure you have permission to publish images, or you will be infringing copyright!

Videos on Facebook

Facebook makes it very simple to add videos to your timeline. You can upload them directly from your PC or mobile device. Alternatively, if you paste the URL of a YouTube or Vimeo video it will automatically configure itself into a rectangular icon in your timeline.

It is a good idea to have an engaging headline for your video along with some form of comment which may make your fans want to view it.

Milestones

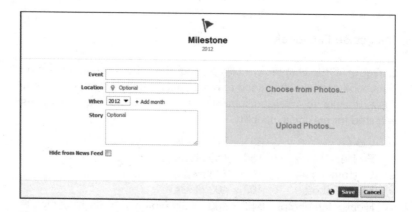

One of the key features of Timeline was the introduction of Milestones. On personal profiles these are known as life events, where you can categorise your life into key personal milestones such as marriage, birth of children, starting a new business etc.

With Pages, the milestones take on a more corporate feel. These form the building blocks of your organisation's timeline. You can fill in the name of an event, the location, the day it happened, include a story and post an image to accompany it.

A great example of this is Manchester United (www.facebook.com/manchesterunited), whose timeline goes all the way back to 1878. Remember that your first milestone **must** be the earliest event in your organisation's history.

Community management

By now, you should be realising that managing a Facebook Page properly can be a time-consuming task, depending on what you would like it to do for you.

Many customer service advisers or technical support teams are now using Pages as a way to communicate with customers.

Example

Vodafone UK has a Got a Question app where users can get answers to specific issues. Named customer service advisers deal with the questions privately, in contrast to the conversations taking place on the Page's timeline.

Smaller brands who use their Facebook Page as the central plank within their marketing strategy may find that the part-time role they had envisaged for managing the Page turns into a full-time community management job.

If you do appoint a community manager, whether internally or filling a new post through recruitment, you need to revisit the guidelines at the beginning of this chapter and also define the role clearly with a proper strategy. Some of the questions you may need to ask yourself before going down the community management route are:.

- Who will administer the Page and what level of access do they need?
- How much time should be devoted to managing the Page?
- What are the 'lines to take' if negative comments are posted? What's our escalation plan?
- Who will monitor the Page outside of office hours?
- What are the lines of authorisation when replying to people on the Page?

If you have a product or service where you know you are likely to have a high number of complainants – local authorities, utilities companies, major brands – it is best to employ traditional brand protection techniques. The key one here would be to take those complaining off the Facebook Page and deal with them directly through a phone conversation or email.

We would recommend using the same customer service techniques as suggested in our chapter on Twitter.

Case study: Petnet360

An excellent UK example of how to use Facebook cleverly for business is Petnet360, which runs the successful Park Bench (www.facebook.com/joinparkbench) and Scratching Post (www.facebook.com/joinscratchingpost) Pages. Petnet360 is an online portal backed by an experienced veterinary company that wants dog and cat owners to have fun bringing up their animals and that promotes good health.

It has a clear mission – to grow its two brands by building engaged communities of dog and cat lovers. Great content, clever use of polls, regular questions and intelligent use of apps mean that a high proportion of its fans regularly engage with the Pages.

One of the key messages of social media is that you do **not** directly sell. Instead, you create the conditions by which people naturally want to do business with you. And Petnet360 is an excellent example of this.

Rather than talk about the veterinary services it has to offer and directly selling animal products, first and foremost the company engages with its communities, educating and informing as well as entertaining its fans – many of whom naturally go on to use its services and buy its products. Furthermore, because the Pages are so targeted towards dog and cat lovers, other companies will pay Petnet360 for the chance to showcase their products.

So, the company does actually make money in three different ways, without directly selling to its customer base.

Facebook apps

As well as tabs within Pages, which direct users to specific applications, it is possible to create stand-alone applications within Facebook itself. These programs sit within the site and are added to individual users' personal profiles. Games such as Farmville and Angry Birds can be played within Facebook.

Working with specific app designers, you can create your own programs, which could in themselves raise your visibility on the site and encourage sharing. For more details check out Facebook's page – http://developers.facebook.com/docs/guides/canvas/.

Facebook deals

Taking a leaf out of Foursquare's book (see Chapter 10), Facebook has introduced its own way of allowing brands to reward fans who check in to different locations.

There are four types of deal on offer for Pages:

1. individual: individuals
2. friend: groups of customers
3. loyalty: rewarding loyal customers
4. charity: donate to charities each time customers check in.

Here is a video that Facebook has produced which outlines how these work – www.facebook.com/video/video.php?v=10100211990206733.

Using targeted advertising on Facebook

Up until the early part of 2012, it was perfectly possible to be visible on Facebook simply by putting into action everything we have outlined in this chapter.

However, with the advent of Timeline, the influence of EdgeRank and the move to a more mobile platform for Facebook, it is now increasingly difficult to meet specific business objectives on the site without setting aside some form of promotional budget.

Following the IPO in 2012, Facebook has had to tread a fine line between turning in a healthy profit and staying true to its original roots. This has meant the appearance of adverts in news feeds on both PC and mobile versions of the site. At the same time, many organisations have found that the only way they can overcome EdgeRank and reach even their existing fan base is by spending money.

There are four main ways in which you can improve your visibility on Facebook using paid-for methods of marketing. Most depend on demographic targeting and pay-per-click (PPC) advertising. This works in a similar way to Google AdWords whereby you create an online advertisement and pay each time a user clicks on it.

Display ads (appear on the right-hand side of the screen on computers)

A business creates an ad and pays Facebook to deliver it to a targeted audience using PPC. For example, you might see an ad for a local gym, if you are of a certain age and like running.

A full list of the demographic criteria is below. Depending on where you wish to run a campaign, Facebook will start off with the total population of the country/countries on the site, then narrow the figure as you introduce more of these criteria:

- location – country, state or town
- age
- gender
- precise interests
- broad categories e.g. movie/film, retail/shopping, sports
- sub categories e.g. Bollywood movies, luxury goods, golf
- connections
- friends of connections
- interested in
- relationship status
- languages
- education
- workplaces.

This method of advertising is a great way to increase the Likes on your Page or to drive traffic to specific web pages.

Sponsored stories (appear in news feeds on mobile and PC versions)

A sponsored story is different from a display ad because it's a story you can already see, about activity from people you're connected to, Pages you like or apps you use. A business pays to sponsor these regular stories to increase the chances that you'll notice it. You can find more on this here: www.facebook.com/video/video. php?v=10100328087082670.

These work well when you want to ensure a more targeted audience for your content.

Promoted posts (appear within news feeds on mobile devices)

Once your Page has 100 Likes, you can promote your content (be it photo, video, link or poll) to your existing fan base or their friends on Facebook. This can cost anywhere between $5 and $100 depending on how many Likes your Page has and how large the target audience is. More information on this can be found here: www.facebook.com/help/ promote.

These are effective at increasing the visibility of your posts to your existing fan base.

Targeted posts

These are a more focused version of promoted posts. Pages with more than 5,000 Likes (correct as of March 2013) can target their updates to a specific audience based on seven different sets of criteria: gender, relationship status, education status, interested in, age, location and language. You can read more here: http://bit.ly/WTxJwt.

These posts ensure you can target your content directly to people who are likely to be interested in what you have to say.

Plan, target and measure your chosen approach

With all these approaches, as with any other form of advertising cam-paign, it is important that you plan properly, think about your target demographic and make sure you have a well-worded ad. At the same time, you must ensure that your Facebook Page or appropriate landing page is optimised so that when people visit it, they find what they are looking for.

With all forms of pay-per-click advertising, whether on Google, LinkedIn or Facebook, you also need to plan when you want your ad to appear, set the correct budget for your campaign and keep measuring the results, using Google Analytics and Facebook Insights.

For more on the subject, check out this one-hour webinar, which talks about using advertising on Facebook to drive engagement and sales: http://youtu.be/X_qa0O7T-V0.

Social media marketing action plan

- Think about what exactly you want to use a Facebook Page for. If there is no specific objective, you may be wasting your time.
- You also need to ask yourself whether you have a natural community of fans who are likely to engage with your Page. Clearly, some organisations are more social than others.
- Put as much energy into your Page as you would into your website. Don't think of it as a gimmicky add-on – in some cases it could end up as your main online presence. You may also need to consider setting up an account with an online photo library.
- Think carefully about who will administer your Page and what level of access you will grant to people.
- Decide who will 'community manage' it. That part-time role you envisaged may end up being almost full time for some organisations. There's nothing more pointless than a Page that is rarely updated or never responds to comments.
- Be creative in getting people to Like and engage with your Page. You need to have a specific plan of action. We believe in a return to old-fashioned customer service: engaging with your customers and finding out what they think about your products.
- Think about using Facebook advertising as a way to build your visibility on the site.
- And finally – be creative. Content is king – especially on Facebook!

6 | YouTube: the future of online content

> What you will learn from this chapter:
>
> - Why video is so important
> - How to fit video into your marketing strategy
> - Uses for video
> - Shooting videos
> - Setting up and managing a YouTube channel
> - Promoting your videos
> - Measuring the performance of your channel

Many people will be surprised to learn that by the end of 2011, over half of *all* global consumer internet traffic was video. Furthermore, Cisco Systems (http://blogs.cisco.com/ar/cisco-visual-networking-index-new-findings) has estimated that by 2016, the sum of all forms of video (TV, video on demand, internet, and sites like YouTube) will be approximately **86% of global consumer traffic**.

According to recent research from ComScore (www.comscore.com/Insights/Press_Releases/2011/12/More_than_200_Billion_Online_Videos_Viewed_Globally_in_October), 1.2 billion people aged 15 or older watched 201.4 billion videos during one month! And as global broadband connectivity rises, it's estimated that the content we consume online will be dominated by video.

In fact 90% of the UK's web-using population already watch video as part of their online activity. YouTube dominates video consumption at 48%, followed by Facebook at 27%. In Europe, ComScore reported that Italy, Spain and France all have a faster-growing video audience than the UK or the USA (http://bit.ly/NjaxU4). The latest research by ComScore (http://bit.ly/PJfxiT) also shows that there is a high penetration of online video in countries in the Asia Pacific region, including Taiwan, Vietnam, Indonesia and the Philippines.

Clearly, as a platform, video is not to be ignored. The question is, how do businesses use video smartly to assist in brand awareness and, ultimately, new business development?

A recent study by Search Engine Land illuminated the power of video by posing the question, "Which of the following have you ever done as a result of viewing an online video ad?" The responses were:

- took action after seeing video ad – 52%
- elicited a response – 45%
- looked for more information – 28%
- bought something – 18%.

In a nutshell, video is big news and likely to become an important part of any organisation's marketing strategy. At the heart of this video revolution is YouTube, although there are several other platforms which allow users to generate and share their own content.

As with so many other aspects of the social media revolution, it has been changes in technology that have enabled video to be used so successfully. Five or 10 years ago, using video in your digital marketing strategy would have been out of the reach of all but the largest organisations.

Three key drivers have made video a viable option. First came the digitisation of film, allowing video to be made much more 'portable'. Next, better internet bandwidth and speeds enabled moving images to be featured online without crashing websites or taking hours to load. Finally, mobile technology means that anyone can not only shoot video via their phone but also broadcast it using social media.

The result is that now, with a decent level of ingenuity, virtually any organisation can incorporate moving images into their marketing mix. Many smartphones have perfectly acceptable video cameras, and there are a host of accessories on the market that make shooting film easy. The choice of video editing programmes and apps (many of which are free) to help you make professional-looking footage continues to grow. Such is the importance of video that some organisations are even setting aside rooms in their offices to create home-grown 'studios'.

The platform that best epitomises how important video has become is YouTube, which was officially launched in November 2005 as a simple video-sharing site. Over the past seven years it has grown exponentially into a media giant. Taken over by Google in November 2006, YouTube is now the third most-visited website in the world as well as the second most-visited search engine (after Google). If Facebook has the potential to become the new newspaper, YouTube has the assets to take over from TV as the prime source of moving images. According to its own figures, four billion videos are streamed daily, while 72 hours of fresh content is uploaded every minute by YouTube's 500 million user base. The introduction of live streaming, the integration with view-on-demand sites like BBC iPlayer and 4OD, plus the ability to rent and watch full-length movies, means that YouTube has become a broadcasting giant. In addition, the site's integration with Google+, as well as Google itself, means that many organisations can dramatically improve their online visibility by having a presence on YouTube (in the context of an overall search engine optimisation strategy).

However, YouTube is by no means the only online video-sharing site. Vimeo (www.vimeo.com) actually pre-dates YouTube and is a popular site used by film makers and the creative industry. Viddy (www.viddy.com) and Socialcam (www.socialcam.com) are video applications built around mobile devices, while Telly.com (formerly www.Twitvid.com) and, more recently, Twitter's 'Vine' are a great ways of sharing videos on Twitter. In China, where YouTube is not widely available, the key video-sharing site is Youku (www.youku.com), while many countries have their own home-grown sites: for example, India has IndiaPad (www.indianpad.in), Germany has MyVideo (www.myvideo.de) and France has Wideo (www.wideo.fr).

There are also sites like Animoto (www.animoto.com) where you can very simply create and manage your own videos from photographs, slides and existing videos. These can then be uploaded to one of the video-sharing sites or other social networks to reach the desired audience.

The majority of these sites are compatible with Facebook, while YouTube and Vimeo can easily be integrated with websites, via WordPress or other content management systems.

In the age of mobile internet, all of these sites are available as apps, ensuring that it is not only easy to make film but also simple to edit it and distribute it by using the range of social networks on offer. In fact, the first images to come out of Haiti after the devastating earthquake there in 2010 were video images posted on Twitter – footage that was then quickly used by news agencies around the world.

Integrating video into your marketing strategy

Like any other social network, before you create a presence on YouTube or any of the other video-sharing sites, it is important to examine your business objectives. How will video help you achieve your goals and how will you go about creating a defined video content strategy?

While it may be practically free to shoot video, and in many cases this is the desirable option, there may be occasions when you need to allocate a budget to create something a little more professional. Just as, in theory, anyone can take a photograph, but very few people shoot like Annie Leibovitz, the same is true of video and it can often be more cost-effective to bring in specialists. Also, is there a 'video-friendly' culture in your organisation? One of the purposes of using video is to humanise your brand. If your employees would rather not appear in front of a camera or are very uncomfortable doing so, you will fail in your attempts to show the human face of your company.

For many organisations, using video is a major step forward and one that may never have been considered before, because of the technological issues and costs associated with it. Part of a marketer's challenge is to help create a more open culture, where people feel at home on screen and understand video's enormous benefits.

The first step could be to alter your website so that video content can easily be uploaded. As stated earlier, most content management systems now have easy-to-use modules. However, as with blogs, once you have committed yourself to showcasing video, you need to have a proper strategy in place to ensure that you can feed the channel on a regular basis. If you do manage to upload videos to either your home page or a landing page, you will be rewarded, not just from giving visitors to your site a more rounded view of your brand, but also from search engines. Google is always on the lookout for fresh content and videos rank very highly, especially when they are properly tagged.

Ways of using video

Organisations may well be interested in principle in using video but a lack of experience in using the medium may give them a fairly blinkered view on its uses – people often assume that video is best suited to creative industries. When video is used, too often there are too many 'talking heads' – people from an organisation sitting behind a desk delivering a monologue that has neither been thought through nor properly executed. Marketing is all about innovation and trying to do things differently. Now that video is an affordable and easily accessible marketing option, it is time to try to do things a little differently.

> ### Case study: Dollar Shave Club
>
> A great example of this is a video posted by Dollar Shave Club on YouTube in 2012 (www.youtube.com/DollarShaveClub). At the time of writing it has had well over 9½ million views. This clip will prove to you that if it is done well, video can assist a wide range of industries, professions and sectors.
>
> In the video, which cost just $4,500 to make, the CEO of Dollar Shave Club (www.dollarshaveclub.com), an SME that ships razors for as little a dollar a month, appeared in a 94-second clip, along with one of his employees, to advertise his products.
>
> The result was that this small start-up with just five members of staff dramatically increased its brand awareness, signed up thousands of new customers and even attracted over $1 million of venture capital funding.

As with all other aspects of marketing, it really pays to be creative. If someone selling razor blades can get over nine million views of a video, why can't you? So here are a few ideas to get you thinking about how you could use video to achieve your business goals.

Promotional films

In the past, organisations with reasonable marketing budgets may have set aside money to shoot promotional videos. The issue was how to distribute these to potential customers. Now, videos can easily be incorporated into websites, email signatures, documents and, of course, blogs, as well as social media sites. It is rare that these are produced in house but they can be, and the cost may be less than other forms of marketing such as brochures and sponsorship.

> ### Example
> Birkbeck College, University of London, has produced a short promotional video to advertise the courses it offers: www.youtube.com/BirkbeckVideo.

Testimonials/interviews with customers

These days, it's not what *you* say about your products or services that matters, but what others are saying about them. Ninety-two per cent of consumers around the world say they trust earned media, such as word of mouth and recommendations from friends and family, above all other forms of advertising (www.nielsen.com/us/en/insights/press-room/2012/nielsen-global-consumers-trust-in-earned-advertising-grows.html).

One of the best ways of building trust is to get your customers or clients to talk about the level of service they have received from you. A 30-second clip filmed with a digital camera or smartphone will suffice. The fact that it is not professionally made will make it look that much more authentic and believable.

> ### Example
> Seaspray Hotel in Brighton is a small family-run hotel which has successfully used video on the homepage of their website to build their brand: www.youtube.com/watch?v=Ok1H_8xUPgo.

Interviews with Staff

People buy from people, so it is important to get across the human side of your business to customers. Most websites list their employees and may include photographs of them. However, film provides a 'real world' experience and reveals more of people's character.

It is not just service industries where this is important but also professional services, and the creative and educational sectors. In fact, we've yet to come across an organisation we've worked with or trained where video isn't appropriate to give a three-dimensional view of employees. Often, this may be the difference between a potential customer choosing to use you rather than your competitor.

Short 'how-to' films

How many people have struggled to put together a children's toy or flatpack furniture? Instructions are often unclear or nonexistent. However, a short video clip can often make the user experience that much simpler, as in this film about putting up an IKEA shelf: www.youtube.com/watch?v=yAzSgqe_e_A. Software demonstrations, how a product or service works – video provides a compelling and useful platform to convey instructions and insight.

Using humour to talk about a dry subject

As with the Dollar Shave Club video, it is often a great idea to use humour to make video clips more engaging. Done well, it can turn even the dourest subject into something that viewers will actually want to watch.

Blendtec (www.blendtec.com), manufacturers of blenders, have been very successful in promoting their products via their YouTube channel (www.youtube.com/Blendtec). With millions of video views and over 423,000 channel subscribers, their videos have acquired cult status.

Video press releases/video blogs

Journalists and bloggers, like the rest of us, are increasingly time poor and bombarded by the written word. Very often, a short video press release or blog can be the best way to attract their attention and help you to stand out from the crowd. At the same time, fresh video content added to your website will help boost your rankings on search engines.

Thought leadership

One of the objectives of using video is to raise the profile of key members of staff or to build thought leadership in a given sector. Keynote speeches or presentations are often an excellent environment for people to shine, so they make great content for videos. Similarly, showcasing your knowledge about a specific area is a key way to build thought leadership. And video can be a powerful way of discussing and providing insight into complex matters that are difficult or dry to explain in writing.

Example

Here is a clip from Sharma Solicitors in which one of their partners talks about unfair dismissal. You'll see that it's had several thousand views and ranks highly on YouTube's search for the keywords 'unfair dismissal uk': http://youtu.be/sUJKWsZsAFU

Podcasts/vodcasts

Sound (podcast) or video (vodcast) clips are an excellent way to get your message across or build your brand. They are listened to or watched primarily on mobile devices, and users can also subscribe to the broadcasts, enabling organisations to build a community of engaged followers.

Example

The global management consulting firm Hay Group (www.haygroup. com) includes a number of podcasts and vodcasts on their site as well as videos on their YouTube channel: www.youtube.com/ HayGroupVideos.

Leverage video-building applications such as Animoto

There are some clever online applications which make it possible to turn slides, pictures and videos into something which looks pretty professional. Using apps such as Animoto, within just a few minutes we were able to turn a PowerPoint presentation into a short promotional video: www.youtube.com/watch?v=RemjwzND4yQ&feature=context-chv

FAQs

If you provide products or services and host a page on your website that covers your FAQs, then you could create videos that address the main points of most queries. Often film can get the message across succinctly and clearly.

'About Us'

If you have a website, you probably have an About Us page. If you look at your web analytics, it's likely you'll see that About Us is a quite regularly visited page. Think about your own web habits. If you are researching a new provider or a product or service online, you're likely to go to the About Us page to see who the people are behind the business. Consider bringing your About Us page to life by including video that really does highlight who you are and what you do.

Sales

It is a myth that you cannot sell via social media. Remember: it's about creating the conditions to get people to know you, like you, trust you and, ultimately, do business with you. Video is no exception. As with Facebook, many organisations are now using video AdWords to promote their brand, product or services.

According to ComScore, in 2012 in the USA consumers found online video ads to be 38% more memorable than ads on traditional television – see more on this here: www.comscore.com/Insights/Presentations_ and_Whitepapers/2012/2012_US_Digital_Future_in_Focus.

The huge volume of people now accessing YouTube, plus the integration of Google's pay-per-click system into video, means that it is now possible to get your message across to a large, targeted group of customers.

Here is a useful video from YouTube which explains how you can advertise directly using the site: www.google.co.uk/ads/video.

You can also leverage video to build a fan base and showcase your wares. Singer Ed Sheeran (www.youtube.com/user/EdSheeran) quickly grew a fan base online using YouTube. He built up a subscriber list of over 300,000 people and had millions of video views, which enabled him to shift thousands of albums.

Creating videos

Once you have decided that you want to use video as part of your marketing strategy and have highlighted the applications that will best meet your business needs, you need to think about actually creating the videos.

Whether you decide to shoot the video yourself or get professionals in to do it for you, it is vital that you prepare a brief. Here are some ideas of what you need to include in your brief.

- **What is the key message you want to convey?** Ideally, focus on just one or two messages. More than that and you run the risk of muddying the waters.
- **What do you want the video to achieve?** There has to be a *reason* for doing the video – brand building, thought leadership, increased sales or better customer engagement, for example.
- **Who is it aimed at?** As with all forms of marketing, think about your target audience(s). Put yourself in their shoes and try to imagine what would appeal to them.
- **What is your call to action?** As with other forms of online marketing, such as websites, AdWords and blogs, you want viewers to do something after watching the video. Do you want them to go to your website, call you, email you?
- **Who will appear in the video?** Whoever you choose to be in the clip must be a) willing and b) able to deliver a performance that will do your brand justice. Warning: This may not be the CEO.
- **What sort of budget are you going to set aside?** This goes not just for individual videos but for creating a regular supply of dynamic footage.
- **Where and when are you going to shoot the video?** Do you have a suitable location?

Creating a storyboard and writing a script

The next step is to prepare your storyboard. Looking rather like a set of PowerPoint slides, this will be a rough diagram giving you an idea about what you will be filming. It will contain the different scenes to be shot. Like any good story, there should be a beginning (introduction), middle (key message) and end (conclusion plus call to action).

> **Example**
>
> Here is a great video by Howcast (www.howcast.com) showing how to prepare a storyboard: http://youtu.be/65_3bq_0eSY

Very few of us can deliver pithy, off-the-cuff performances in front of camera. Even seasoned speakers or actors need some form of basic script or cue cards in order to put on the optimum performance. So once you have a storyboard prepared, you should write some form of script. This can either be memorised or cue cards can be held up by a colleague/assistant when filming. The result will be a smooth and professional-looking video rather than a stilted and amateur one.

With your storyboard and script prepared, you are ready to film your video. Here are some handy pointers.

- Make sure that your camera is in focus and there is enough light. You may want to purchase or hire extra lighting.
- Think about investing in a clip-on microphone to ensure optimum sound quality.
- Use a tripod or other form of rest to eradicate camera shake.
- Think about the background and make sure that where you are filming is neat and tidy – and appropriate.
- Ensure that the subject of your film is dressed appropriately. If you are going to film several videos in one day they will need a change of clothes, accessories, etc.

Editing your video

Statistics show that 33% of viewers watch only the first 30 seconds of videos, another 11% lose interest and leave at the one-minute mark, and altogether 60% bail out after just two minutes. So, however much footage you have, it is important to edit it down, ideally to two minutes or less, and ensure that the first 30 seconds covers your key message and is compelling to encourage users to carry on watching.

There are a range of video editing tools, many of which are free, including YouTube's own video editor (www.youtube.com/editor). There are also paid-for programmes such as iMovie (www.apple.com/ilife/imovie), Sony Vegas Movie Studio (www.sonycreativesoftware.com/moviestudiope), Microsoft's Movie Maker (www.microsoft.com/education/moviemaker) and Roxio Creator (www.roxio.com).

All these programs allow you to add sound, overlays, subtitles and special effects, all of which will enhance the final video and give it a professional feel.

There are some fabulous apps out there too. We particularly like Frameographer, which enables time lapse and stop motion movies on your iPhone (www.studioneat.com/products/frameographer).

Setting up your YouTube channel

Now you have a video or a set of videos to upload, you can think about setting up your own YouTube channel. Remember, this may be one of the key ways in which your organisation or company stays visible online, so take your time in making it look the best it can.

Here are the steps to take to get your channel set up.

1. Go to www.youtube.com/signup. You will be asked to create a stand-alone Google account. This is used to log in to YouTube. We recommend that you use something like *yourcompanynamevideos @gmail.com* as the email address. Remember to make a note of the password.

2. Back in YouTube, click on Upload in the top right-hand corner of the screen. You will then be asked to choose a username. As with Facebook, it is a good idea to choose either a brand-specific or a keyword-rich name. For example, the well-known brand Marks & Spencer has www.youtube.com/marksandspencertv (brand focus), while St Albans plumber Ryan Moffat has www.youtube.com/plumbersinstalbans (keyword focus).

3. Customise your channel. The first step is to go to Channel Settings and hit the Appearance tab. You can now upload your company or organisation's logo. As with Facebook, you need to ensure that the logo fits the avatar window, so we recommend that you use the same avatar as you would on Facebook (180 × 180 pixels in size).

4. At the same time you can change the background of the channel. Like your Facebook timeline, you need to ensure that this is of a high enough quality to entice viewers. You can upload a photograph or design a custom background if you have nothing suitable. Note that this background image needs to fit the standard YouTube channel presets, so you can either engage the services of a designer or download one of the many templates available online.

5. Next, click on the Info and Settings tab and fill in a succinct and, ideally, keyword-enabled 'boilerplate' that sums up the purpose of your business or organisation.

6. To choose the format in which you want to showcase the videos you have on your channel, stay within Channel Settings and hit Tabs. You will then need to check the 'Featured' box. This will give you a range of options to help you alter the layout of your site.

7. Be social! Remember that YouTube is a social network and you want to engage with the people viewing your videos. Make sure that in your account settings, you enable the Comment setting.

8. Subscribe to other channels. In Facebook, when administering your Page, you can Like the Pages of partner organisations or companies you want to be associated with. The same is true of YouTube. Search for the organisations and companies whose videos you would like to feature on your channel, hit the Subscribe button and these will start to appear in your news feed.

9. By Liking videos, these will appear in your news feed. Think of your channel as being your own TV station. Some of the content you will produce yourself; and you will broadcast entire series (subscribing) as well as one-off programmes (Likes). Like a TV station, you

want your content to be engaging, of interest to casual visitors and subscribers alike, as well as informative. Remember that there may well be occasions when your YouTube channel is where you want to drive traffic to.

10. Create playlists. Like lists in Twitter, these are a great way to categorise the videos that you have featured on your channel. Go to Video Manager and click on the Playlists tab. Then click on view playlist. Once you have playlists, when you are viewing videos, you can not only Like them but also add them to a specific playlist. You can also create a playlist when viewing videos – either on a PC or on a mobile device via the YouTube app. There is of course a Favorites list which you can also add videos to. This is similar to favouriting tweets.

Uploading videos and managing your channel

You should now have a fully functioning channel as well as the means to create your own videos. Finally, you are now in a position to start uploading videos. This is a very simple process. Log in to your YouTube account and in the top right-hand corner of the page you will see the Upload tab.

You are then presented with three options.

1. You can upload a file straight from your PC or tablet device.
2. You can upload multiple files.
3. You can record live via webcam.

Note: There is a 15-minute limit for videos and the file size is limited to 2GB for uploads from YouTube's website or 20GB if up-to-date browser versions are used. For more information see YouTube's guidelines:

http://support.google.com/youtube/bin/answer.py?hl=en&answer=71673

Showcasing your video

However you decide to upload your video, once it is on YouTube you need to ensure that it gets maximum visibility on the site. Here are some tips.

- Just as newspaper headlines are used to grab people's attention, it is important that you give your video a great title. Make it catchy and include some of your keywords. For example, West London Accountants BOSS have a channel called www.youtube.com/accountantwestlondon as well as titling their video with the key-

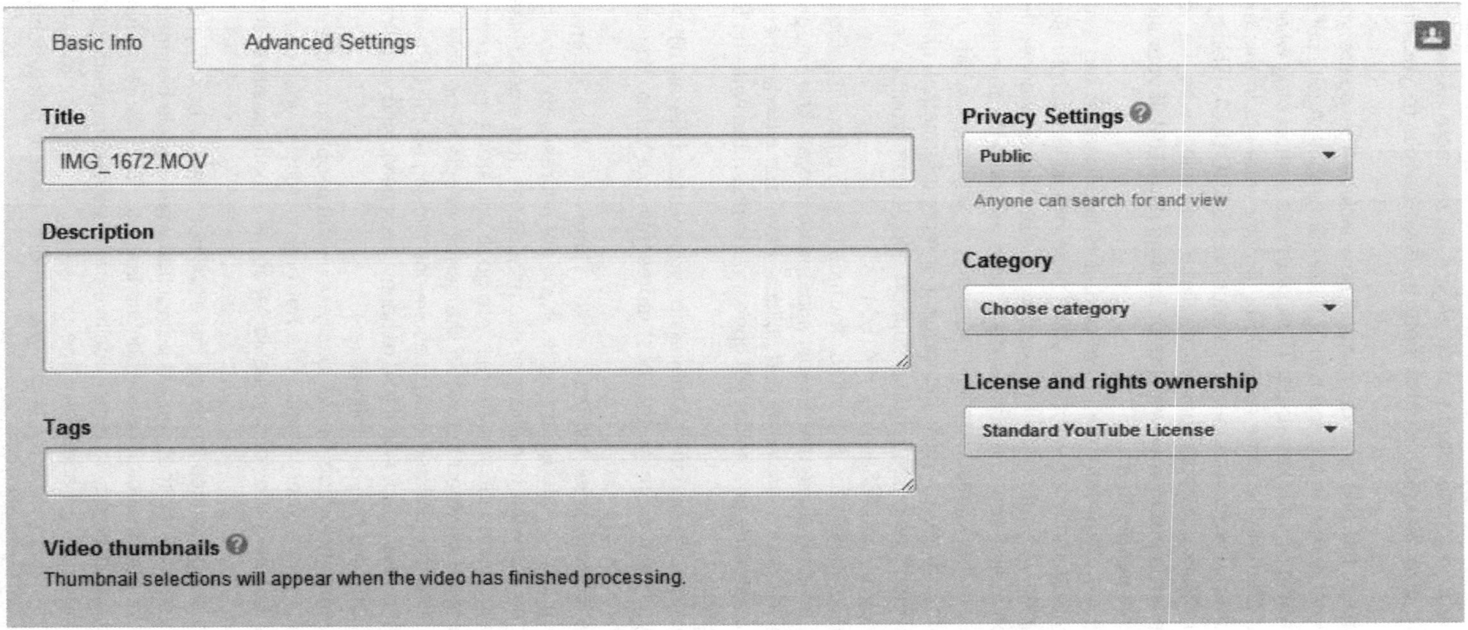

Basic Info | Advanced Settings

Title

IMG_1672.MOV

Description

Tags

Privacy Settings ?

Public

Anyone can search for and view

Category

Choose category

License and rights ownership

Standard YouTube License

Video thumbnails ?

Thumbnail selections will appear when the video has finished processing.

words 'West' 'London' and 'accountants'. Remember that YouTube is the second most visited search engine, so the more assistance you can give Google's search bots to drive people to you, the better.

- Underneath the title is a description box. Include the points you want to get across in the first two or three paragraphs. Again, put in a smattering of your keywords. Think of this as a short blog where there is a strong headline followed by a pithy write-up. In this example (http://www.youtube.com/watch?v=5Cll0pD1lo8), Chicago butcher Mark Holzkopf has three lines explaining who he is. **Remember to put in your website or landing page URL if your aim is to drive people there**.

- As with metatags within your website, it is important to tag your video with as many keywords as you can as well as words/phrases which relate to your product or service. This box appears under the description and you can add as many tags as you wish to ensure you reach the widest possible audience – similar to what you would do with an AdWords campaign. For more information, check out YouTube's help page: http://support.google.com/youtube/bin/answer.py?hl=en-GB&answer=141804.

- Choose a category for your video. YouTube has 15 different categories, so select the one that is most appropriate for you. The categories include education, news and politics, travel and entertainment, etc. The category you select will appear underneath the write-up to your video.

- Choose the appropriate thumbnail for your video. Like an album cover, you want an image that best represents your video. You are given a choice of three.

- Set the privacy level for your video. There are three different levels – public, unlisted and private. If you are not ready to 'publish' your video and want to make changes or additions, it is a good idea to keep it private until you are ready to go. If you aren't quite ready to promote your video but would like certain people to be able to see it, go for the unlisted option, as anyone clicking on the URL will be taken to the video. And if you're happy, click public and your first video will be live on your channel.

- Check regularly for comments. Ideally, you want people to comment on and/or share your videos. This not only increases your online visibility but also provides valuable feedback – both positive and negative.

Note: It is a good idea to check the email notifications box in your account settings so that you will be notified when people comment on your videos or subscribe to your channel, etc. It is important that you respond promptly to either positive or negative comments, just as you would on a Facebook Page or Twitter. As with any form of online or offline media relations, you need to have in place some procedures for dealing with negative comments.

- It is worth noting that the more comments and shares you get, the more likely you are to appear in YouTube's search and therefore in Google's. As with all forms of online marketing, fresh, relevant content gets rewarded by higher search rankings.
- You can post on your wall, as you would on Facebook or LinkedIn. This is another way to add content and also a great way to draw attention to new videos or playlists that you think may be of interest to your channel subscribers.

Promoting your videos

While your YouTube channel provides a great online focus for all your videos, you need to think about a strategy to promote both your videos and your channel. Just as over 40% of UK websites get no traffic and many blogs remain unseen, a whole range of well-crafted and content-rich videos never see the light of day because they are not adequately promoted.

There are two key ways in which you can promote your videos: organically, via blogs, other social media sites and word of mouth; or the paid-for route of AdWords.

One of the key drivers in the growth of video usage in marketing was digitisation of film. Moving one step further, once you have uploaded a video to YouTube, it will then have its own customised URL. This makes it highly portable and enables you to utilise it in a wide range of media.

Organic promotion

It is important that you try to promote your new video to the widest possible audience. Depending on your audience, we recommend that you think about the best channels to use to promote your video.

For example, if you are a boutique hotel, you could employ an array of marketing devices such as posting the video on your Facebook Page and pinning it to the top of your timeline, posting regular tweets with the link to your video, incorporating it into your blog or using it within an email campaign. You may even want to look at direct mail with a link to your channel or perhaps a QR code linking directly to the video.

> ### Example
> Hôtel des Académies, Montparnasse: www.youtube.com/hoteldes academies and www.facebook.com/pages/Hotel-des-Academies-et-des-Arts-Paris/ten292191686

If you are a law firm specialising in litigation, you could think about posting the video to your LinkedIn company profile, promoting the link on Twitter, incorporating it into press releases and perhaps even having a module on your website to highlight your latest video clips.

Example

Pannone Solicitors: www.youtube.com/PannoneSolicitors and www.pannone.com/media-centre/videos.

Here are some of the ways in which you can promote your video:

- embedded within Microsoft Office applications – Outlook, Word, Excel, PowerPoint
- on your website or a specialist landing page
- email signatures
- traditional marketing – brochures, adverts, PR, fliers, posters
- email campaigns
- blogs
- Facebook Pages
- Twitter
- LinkedIn personal and company profiles
- Google+ Page
- other social networks – Tumblr, Pinterest, Viddy, Vimeo.

Paid-for promotion

An increasingly viable way of promoting your video is to use Google AdWords for video. This works in very much the same way as it does on Google. The difference is that instead of users seeing an ad you have bought when searching on Google, visitors to YouTube will see a link to your video within the site.

There are four different ways your video ad can appear.

1. In search – this is similar to in Google. Ads appear when you search within YouTube.
2. In display – ads appear in the top right-hand corner of the screen when you click on videos.
3. In stream – ads appear in a box set within a video you are watching.
4. In slate – used for longer videos. Viewers get the choice of three different ads.

With all of these forms of advertising, you pay only when people click on your ad.

For full information on how you could be using ads on YouTube, visit Google's own page: http://www.google.com/ads/video.

Measuring the performance of your videos

One of the mantras in marketing is 'testing and measuring'. Video is no different. You may think that the videos you are posting are great, but if you don't get anyone commenting on them or you don't use the correct promotional strategy to get them out to a wider audience, they will have less value. Using Google Analytics and YouTube's own analytics, it is possible to measure exactly how much engagement there has been with your videos as well as how much traffic has been driven via each of the different places you have promoted your video.

When accessing your channel, at the top right-hand corner of the screen you'll see an Analytics tab. The drop-down menu is shown below. Clicking on this will give you a large amount of data including the demographics of viewers, traffic sources and number of views. The data can be broken down further when linked to an AdWords campaign. In addition, you will be able to gauge the level of interaction that people have had both with your videos and with your channel.

By accessing Google Analytics, you will also be able to measure the amount of traffic that has come to your website or specific landing page via YouTube.

There is a huge amount of data on offer, which can often become overwhelming. It is always a good idea to set four or five key performance indicators (KPIs) so that you can focus on achieving the specific business objectives you set when embarking on a video content marketing strategy for your organisation.

Overview

▾ **Views reports**

Views

Demographics

Playback locations

Traffic sources

Audience retention

▾ **Engagement reports**

Subscribers

Likes and dislikes

Favorites

Comments

Sharing

Annotations (Beta)

Social media marketing action plan

- Think about how you will use a defined video content marketing strategy to help you achieve your business goals.
- Create the right culture in your organisation before going down the video route. Filming people is a huge step forward and can be uncomfortable for many organisations.
- Be creative in how you use video. Don't just go down the tried and tested 'talking heads' route. Remember, marketing is all about innovation.
- Set aside some sort of budget. Whether you decide to shoot videos in house or employ an outside agency, there will be some form of expenditure – even if it is purchasing a camera or smartening up one of the meeting rooms to turn it into an impromptu studio.
- Be proactive. If you are going to have a video channel – on YouTube or one of the other video-sharing sites – ensure that you have a strategy to keep it regularly updated with engaging content.
- Promote your videos so that they reach the widest possible audience. This can be done through organic or paid-for methods.
- Test and measure. Find out what works and what doesn't using Google and YouTube analytics.

7 | LinkedIn

What you will learn from this chapter:

- Background to LinkedIn
- Creating the right personal profile
- Leveraging your contacts
- Ways to engage on the site
- Creating and optimising a company profile
- Understanding LinkedIn Insights
- Engaging via Polls
- Effective lead generation via LinkedIn

LinkedIn is often referred to as 'the professionals' Facebook'. It's the one social network that most people 'get'. Admittedly, we still hear, *'Yes, I have a LinkedIn profile but I'm not sure what to do with it'*, but it's the one social network out of the big four that makes its proposition very clear – 'we're here to do business'.

Over the years, LinkedIn has grown its reputation as being the business to business social network. A study by leading inbound marketing specialists Hubspot (www.hubspot.com) reported that LinkedIn is three times more effective for lead generation than Facebook and Twitter. That makes perfect sense as it's unlikely that you would go to LinkedIn for 'entertainment' value (although their relatively new LinkedIn Today news feature keeps us hooked).

If we were to explain Twitter and Facebook very briefly, we would say something like this.

- **Twitter** is the 'buzziest' social network – a perfect mouthpiece for sharing content and information and connecting and engaging with people you have never met, and will never have the opportunity to meet. It's perfect for capturing conversations, listening in and generating reach and traction.
- **Facebook** is about humanising a brand – the perfect vehicle for creating a community, engaging current audiences and encouraging people to share and hence market to new audiences via viral-worthy campaigns and compelling content, providing the potential to grow audience and awareness. It creates a community of 'fans or advocates' who are willing to share and engage with your brand or business.

And then there's LinkedIn . . .

Well, LinkedIn is quite different. Unlike Twitter or Facebook, where self-promotion isn't really advocated, LinkedIn profiles focus on personal self-promotion and are also about leveraging the contacts you already have to get to the contacts you want to have.

It's a place where you can connect with business associates – colleagues, peers, alumni, prospects, clients and so on. You can watch their activities, see when they move roles, see who they're connected to, reach out to them and ask for recommendations – both for your own work and for connections. It's effectively an online 'network' in the truest traditional sense.

Where it started

LinkedIn started out as mainly a recruitment resource – a place where professionals could share their knowledge and expertise, pitch for new contracts and showcase talents to head-hunters and potential recruiters. Unlike the other big social networks, LinkedIn has a free networking service (which we will concentrate on in this chapter), but it also has a few enterprise services that target people who want to use LinkedIn for specific reasons.

The paid-for options

What do they offer?

Currently, there are three services – for recruiters, sales professionals and job seekers. Each service has a Basic, Standard and Plus version and fees in the UK range from £10.95 to £64.95 per month (with the option of getting a discounted fee should you decide to pay for the year up front).

Our advice is that if your business is in recruitment, headhunting and finding talent, a monthly subscription of just under £65 is a no-brainer.

Similarly, if you are job seeking, the Job Seeker packages enable you to find specific jobs that are on job boards, which aren't publicly visible with the free version. And if you are a sales professional tasked with business development, the paid-for versions enable you to target specific decision-makers.

What do you get for your subscription?

Here are some key add-ons in the paid-for versions (but note: *the features depend on which package you subscribe to*).

- See more profiles when you search.
- Add filters to your searches to make the results more targeted.
- View a full list of those that have reviewed your profile.
- Send InMails – direct emails (some with guaranteed responses).
- See people's full profiles, regardless of whether you are connected to them.

We have a number of friends and colleagues who have secured new roles via LinkedIn – either because they were headhunted or because they were actively job seeking – and it works for that purpose, quite beautifully.

LinkedIn isn't just about recruitment

Of course, as with all of the networks in this book, LinkedIn has evolved, and continues to evolve. Businesses can now create quite sophisticated 'Company Profiles' to showcase products and services as well as connect all their employees. LinkedIn is no longer just about individuals showcasing their talents but another space for businesses to promote their people and their products and services with the intention to engage, meet like-minded individuals via LinkedIn Groups and to grow authority.

It's also becoming expected that you will be able to find someone via LinkedIn. Whenever we meet anyone at a networking event or business meeting, it's a natural habit to visit LinkedIn and review their profile. If relevant, then it's usual practice to send a message to connect. Professionals are now expected to have a presence on LinkedIn.

Creating your personal LinkedIn profile

As with all of the social networks, signing up for a profile is a pretty simple process. Supply your name, email address and password and your account is open. (Remember to document all social networking account login details somewhere, so you've got a back-up/reminder – more on that later.) Then it's a case of entering data and optimising as well as possible.

Before you start, you may want to take a breath and consider exactly what you want to leverage LinkedIn for. For example, are you job hunting, looking for business development opportunities or using your profile as a key platform to showcase your expertise and knowledge to your contacts? Remember – the objective of the channel steers the sentiment of your content.

Given that the majority of consumers now seek out products, services and talent online, being visible online is something that all businesses and individuals need to be thinking about. Having a LinkedIn personal profile is therefore useful, but if it's not 100% complete, it is not fully optimised for you to be found in LinkedIn searches and indeed in other search engines too. And if your profile isn't 100% complete, does that look altogether professional? We don't think so. So be sure to get your profile as complete as possible. It should take you no more than an hour. (We've timed it).

You need to include the following information:

- your industry and location
- your current position (with a description)
- two past positions
- your education
- your skills (a minimum of three)
- a profile photo
- at least 50 connections.

When editing your Profile, you'll see that LinkedIn shows you a profile completeness circle and provides hints on the content that still needs to be completed. **Remember – LinkedIn asks for specific information, but you are completely in control of what you put into each field.**

> ### Hot tip
>
> When adding your content into LinkedIn the editing features are very limited – for example, adding bullet points and emboldening text is not straightforward. We suggest that you create your profile in something like Word, and then paste it into LinkedIn. You'll find that it still loses some of the formatting, but it's a lot better than flat text.

Edit your LinkedIn URL

When you are in editing mode, you will see the Edit Contact Info tab. When you click on this, it includes various places where you can add URLs, Twitter names, etc. And, of course, LinkedIn automatically creates a URL for your LinkedIn profile.

The default URL will look like a whole string of letters and numbers – complete nonsense which doesn't mean anything to anyone. You can simply edit your personal LinkedIn URL at any time – and as long as the terms you want are available, then it's yours. For example, the one in the picture has been edited to /michellecarvill. This now becomes your public URL which you can promote and share on email footers or business cards – to showcase you.

Be sure to add other URLs such as your website, blog or Twitter URLs too. Consider this your 'personal splashpage' where people can find out everything about you that you wish them to know.

Optimise your profile with relevant keywords

Here we are again with those magic keywords – the DNA of your organisation's online visibility. After all, they are the crucial words that people will use to search for you, so make sure that you pepper the content of your LinkedIn profile with relevant keywords. Think about the keywords that you feature in your Professional Headline – you can change these at any time, but remember what your objective in using LinkedIn is and tailor them accordingly. Using the right keywords will not only help people find you more easily when they are doing LinkedIn searches, but it also helps with Google searches too.

Michelle Carvill

Social Media Strategy, Social Media Consultant, Social Media Trainer, Author, Blogger and Highly Experienced Marketer

Slough, United Kingdom | Marketing and Advertising

Current   Founder and Director at Carvill Creative

Remember – first and foremost you are writing for human beings, not search bots, so include your keywords in a relevant and purposeful way. Aim for around 6% of the content to be keywords.

Getting connected

When your profile's complete and ready to roll, you can start connecting.

A great way to start is to explore which of your contacts are already on LinkedIn. Doing this is pretty simple. Visit the Contacts tab in the main bar and you'll see Connections (where you can view all the people you are connected with via LinkedIn) and Add Connections. There are two main options: you can insert contact details one by one; or you can invite your contacts via your email service by uploading a simple CSV/ Excel spreadsheet list.

Once you've uploaded the list, LinkedIn sees which of your contacts are already on LinkedIn and presents you with a list of contacts so that you can review and select the ones you wish to connect with on LinkedIn.

Connecting is then automated – a simple click of the button and you can personalise the default message (which we also suggest you do) – and get connected to your contacts on LinkedIn.

LinkedIn's search facility

Before we move on, it's worth noting that LinkedIn has a very good search facility. Not only can you run general searches such as 'IT Manager Frankfurt', but you can also specify whether you want to search People, Updates, Jobs, Companies, Inbox (which works as an email account) or Groups. So you can be pretty specific about which area you want to search in. There is also an Advanced Search, which sits to the right of that search box – and here you can filter some of the search results. (Although filters are limited in the free version.)

Managing your contacts via LinkedIn

The difference between LinkedIn and a normal database or customer relationship management (CRM) system is that rather than being one way (i.e. you control all the data that goes into it), the content is dynamic. It really is a network in the truest sense of the word. Your contacts are sharing information, updating their profiles and even moving on to new careers and you can see it all happening in real time. This makes LinkedIn a very powerful and dynamic database.

Whenever we meet people in a training course, or business meeting or any other guise – we now naturally look to connect with them on LinkedIn. If someone gives us a business card, rather than leaving it to get dusty in the bottom of a bag or jacket pocket, we automatically go to LinkedIn, search for them and if they are on the platform, we connect. Using LinkedIn this way means that you can keep a constant database of contacts, and if they change roles you haven't lost them: their profile remains on LinkedIn.

LinkedIn has a great little service – LinkedIn Updates – that you can subscribe into via your settings (more on settings shortly). Updates allows you to receive an email each week telling you about what's been happening with your contacts – who they've connected with, new roles, profile updates, etc. If you discover that one of your contacts has moved on to a new role, you could even email that contact to congratulate them. And who knows where they may have moved on to – it could very well be that they've gone to an organisation you've wanted to have discussions with for a while. And if so, you now have a relevant contact to leverage.

Database management is often a big headache for organisations, but managing contacts via LinkedIn can be time-saving, long-lasting and very low maintenance.

Requesting recommendations

Asking people, contacts, colleagues, peers, clients, delegates, etc. for recommendations couldn't be easier on LinkedIn. It's a very simple process, and turns what could be a toe-curling request into an automated process. Simply click your Profile tab and in the drop-down menu you will see Recommendations. You can then simply select which contacts you want to request recommendations from.

In the 'recommendation generation', where people trust what others say about products and services rather than what the brands are saying, growing recommendations grows credibility. In addition, all the extra content pads out your profile, giving you even more chance of being found in searches. And, of course, you can use the recommendations in other marketing materials and on your website. The process is so automated that you can even (should you wish to) follow up on those who have not yet sent their recommendation.

As for the person you are asking for a recommendation, it's simple for them too. They simply have to complete their recommendation and hit Send. You can't edit their recommendation, but you do get to choose whether or not you publish it. Of course, if you think they've omitted a key element you wanted them to get across in their recommendation, there's no reason why you can't go back to them and ask them to amend their recommendation to include it.

Beyond recommendations - the new 'Endorsement' feature

As we've mentioned (several times!), the social platforms are evolving all the time. New user functionalities and additional features are added on a regular basis (see the blog we're running alongside this book – www.thebusinessofbeingsocial.co.uk – which will keep you up to date on all updates, amends and new features).

In September 2012, LinkedIn introduced a new Endorsement feature, whereby people can 'endorse' their connections. Whereas with recommendations, someone has to take time and effort to write some-thing about you, Endorsements enable users to simply click a button to endorse you. If they wish, they can add Skills and Reasons why they are endorsing you.

At the moment, the word on the net about this new feature is mixed. Is it simply too easy to click 'Endorse' – and therefore, is there a credibility issue around how meaningful this new measure is? Let's see how it plays out.

Be human on LinkedIn

People do business with people. And while social networks provide us with clever and leveraged ways of keeping in touch with those in our networks in a more automated way, it's still important that we provide a human touch.

For example, when you are inviting people to connect with you in LinkedIn, don't simply use the default message, *'I'd like to add you to my professional LinkedIn network'*. Research has shown that people are more likely to accept and appreciate the connection if you provide some personal context – and even better if you can explain why you're contacting them and add a reason to connect. For example:

> *Great meeting you at ABC the other day – I'd like to keep in touch by connecting on LinkedIn. Thought it would be good to catch up for a coffee to carry on our discussion as I've been thinking about your proposition and have a number of ideas I'd like to share with you.*

Such a different approach – it's very human, it's authentic and it gives a reason why you want to connect. Not to mention the fact that it helps remind the person how you met.

Don't attempt to spam or directly sell on LinkedIn

Even though LinkedIn enables you to send direct emails to specific indi-viduals, you really should consider how it's going to come across. Peo-ple will disconnect from you in a heartbeat if they think you are using LinkedIn solely to sell your wares. Think of offline networking: you wouldn't start a partnership or conversation by trying to sell someone something in your opening conversation. As with all networks, online or offline, engage with, listen to and nurture your contacts – don't spam them.

If someone is specifically discussing something you have a solution for, by all means engage, but listen in first – don't spam.

Connections

Understanding who is connected to whom

Another key feature of LinkedIn is that you can see how people are connected. When you are searching for a person on LinkedIn, next to their
name you will see '1st', '2nd' or '3rd'.

As you can see below – Pete has a '2nd' next to his name. This tells us
that he's not a direct contact, but someone we are connected to has
connections with him.

LinkedIn then advises you who in your network is connected to Pete so
that you can contact them and ask them to make an introduction. (Just
as you would network in the offline world.)

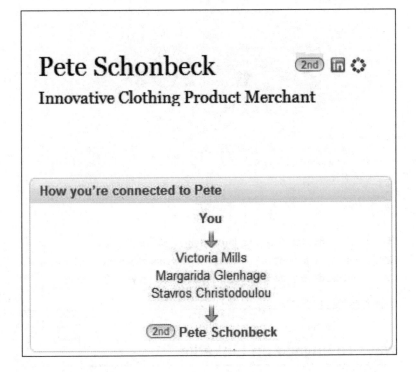

Whenever you search for a person on LinkedIn, you will see these
'degree of connection' numbers – or an 'out of your network' message,
which means that you don't have any related connections directly in
your network.

Using company searches to find relevant connections

If you're looking for someone with whom you don't have any connections you could also try searching for the company they work for.

Their company's LinkedIn profile (more on company profiles later in the chapter) will showcase the company's employees and it may be that other people in the company are connected to you (they could be 1st-, 2nd- or 3rd-degree connections – see the diagram). Therefore, you could work those connections to get introduced to the person you want to connect with.

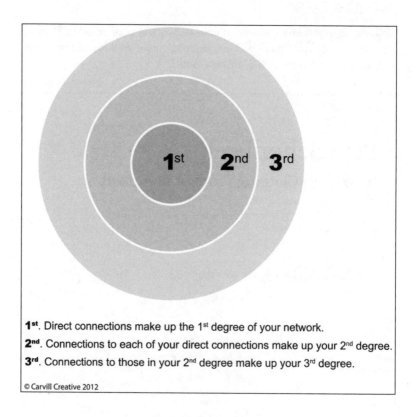

1st. Direct connections make up the 1st degree of your network.

2nd. Connections to each of your direct connections make up your 2nd degree.

3rd. Connections to those in your 2nd degree make up your 3rd degree.

© Carvill Creative 2012

Ways to engage on LinkedIn

LinkedIn groups

LinkedIn groups are effectively mini-networks that assist like-minded people to get involved in relevant discussions and share knowledge, advice and expertise – and, of course, to ask questions. In a group you can add a new topic to a discussion to garner opinion or advice, answer questions from the group members, listen in a passive way or generally interact.

If a group doesn't already exist for the specific topic you want to network around, you can easily create one, search for relevant contacts and people and invite them to that group.

Again, if you're not directly connected to a person you'd really like to participate in the group, you can always see whether any of your connections are, and if so, ask them to invite relevant contacts to the group.

To create a group, review the groups you're already participating in or to get referred to groups, simply see the Groups tab.

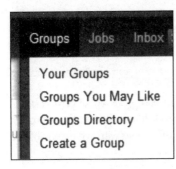

Groups can be a great place to meet like-minded people: they are in effect targeted networking groups. Our advice is to review the groups that fit your objective.

1. Do a simple search of groups and see which ones are relevant to you.
2. Review the types of conversation and engagement in the group. Some people simply go on groups to spam and sell their wares – and as we said earlier, this is never a good networking tactic.
3. Watch and listen. Then, if you think it's the right group for you, join it.

One word of warning: there are groups about groups and you could very quickly become part of many groups. It could be that there is so much noise coming from your groups that you need to tune out (see more on Settings and Privacy later to learn how you can manage the alerts from your groups). Be realistic about the number of groups you can actively participate in. Choose those most fit for purpose and focus attention on the specific groups and people within those groups that meet your objectives.

Create your own hub or intranet

You'll see from the Groups tab that you have the option to create your own group. This is a very simple process. You may want to create a group related to a specific topic (as we discussed earlier) or you may want to create a private group just for a select few. You have the option to create a members-only group, and you could use this as a working hub or an intranet with a select team.

Settings and privacy

Delegates and clients often ask us, 'Will everyone be able to see my connections?' The answer is – that's entirely up to you. LinkedIn has some pretty detailed privacy settings that put you in control of both what you see and what others see about you. As you can see from a screenshot of the privacy settings below, there are a number of elements to consider.

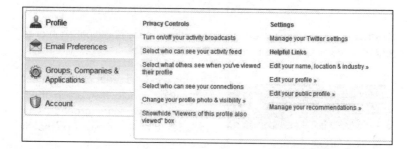

You can manage settings around your profile, your email preferences, group activity and your account in general. It's worth working through each of the settings so that you are comfortable with what's visible to the masses.

> **Hot tip**
>
> When you are updating your profile with new content, we suggest you turn off your activity broadcasts until you have fully completed the new profile. If you keep them on, the broadcasts will circulate to all your connections each time you make a change.

Creating a LinkedIn company profile

Just as with Facebook, you can have a personal profile, which focuses on you, and a brand or company profile that focuses on the business. Having a LinkedIn company profile enables others to learn about what's happening within your business. From news updates to job opportunities, products and services, it's effectively an extension of the information people can find on your website, but it also gives you the opportunity to broadcast status updates to all those following the company.

The LinkedIn company profile provides an opportunity to consolidate the many voices of the business into one centralised voice.

- **Company reach:** the whole team working together to promote both themselves and the business. Win-win.
- **Product/service awareness:** promoting in detail, with relevant keywords, your products and services. Add promos, videos, ads – and get clients/customers to post recommendations.

- **Brand awareness:** the whole team saying the same thing, rather than giving mixed messages. Provide an optimised 'boiler plate' (a simple sentence) for all the team to showcase on their personal profiles, and ensure all the team are connected to the correct company profile.

We'll explore these benefits in more detail later on in the chapter. First, let's look at the practicalities.

Adding a company profile

Before you add a company profile, first check whether one has already been created. Do a simple search on companies and check whether a company profile already exists.

To create a Company Profile, you must have a company domain name-related email address.

> **Example**
>
> To create a company profile for Carvill Creative, we would have to have a company-focused email address such as michelle@carvill creative.co.uk. You can't set up the profile with common email domains such as Gmail, Hotmail or Yahoo!.

With your domain-related email address at the ready, to set up the profile you simply:

1. Click the Companies tab in the top menu, then Add A Company (located to the upper right of the screen).
2. Enter company details and your work-related email address.
3. Click Continue and simply enter all your company information. Remember to optimise with keywords where relevant. Just as people search Google, YouTube, Facebook and Twitter using keywords, so they search LinkedIn. So make sure that you have optimised your online content effectively to give yourself a good chance of being found in relevant searches.

Can anyone create a company profile?

We've mentioned that you have to have a domain-related email address. You also need to have some form of published relationship with the company, which means that you should clearly indicate in your personal profile that you work for the company. And before you can create a company profile, your own personal LinkedIn profile must be more than 50% complete.

Connecting employees to a company profile

When an employee includes the company they work for in their personal profile, their personal profile will automatically connect with the company profile (if it exists). If an employee is not connected, they may have misspelt the company name or they may need to manually connect to the company profile. This is a very simple process. They need to edit their profile, click 'Change Company' next to their 'Current Position' and type the full company name. The company name will appear in a drop-down box, so make sure that your employee is connecting with the correct company. Once that's all done, simply click 'Update'.

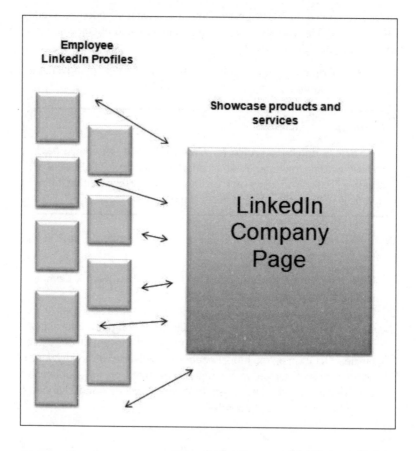

Of course, connecting all your employees to your company profile provides a dual marketing resource for the business. Think about the power of LinkedIn and the ability to see who is connected to whom.

- Let's say a company has 10 employees.
- Each employee has their own personal LinkedIn profile.
- Each employee has 100 1st-degree connections – and of course their connections have connections.

One account of 358 1st-degree connections actually reaches (through the 2nd- and 3rd-degree connections) a whopping 6,655,080 profes-

sionals. Let's be conservative and say that 100 1st-degree connections links to 2,000,000 professionals. With a team of just 10, even with some potential duplication of connections, you can see how amplified the reach of the company's network becomes.

The employee becomes a marketing portal for the business

When someone checks out one of your employees, not only do they get to see their profile, they also get the opportunity to link to the company profile, to find out more about what the company does. Therefore, it makes sense for companies to create a company profile and encourage the whole team to create personal profiles and connect with relevant connections.

This broadens the network – and provides more opportunity for referral and leveraging those we know in order to get to those we want to know.

Setting administrators of the company profile

When setting up the company profile you have two options: to let all employees administer the profile; or to specify which employees are administrators.

As an administrator of a profile, when you search for the company profile you'll see 'Admin Tools' in the far right-hand corner. This button enables you to access the company profile and update accordingly. (This isn't visible unless you are the owner or administrator of the page.)

Optimising your LinkedIn company profile

Once you've got a company profile in place there are a number of tabs you can use to fill it out. Let's take a look at each in more detail.

Company overview

In September 2012 LinkedIn showcased a change to their company profiles. This change enables companies to include a 'cover shot'-style header in their overview section. A company profile with cover shot looks pretty similar to a Facebook Page cover shot.

The overview is going to be the first port of call for visitors, so it's where you should showcase your company's boilerplate – when it was established, partners, clients, etc. This is similar to the 'About Us' section of your website. Remember – people are more interested in what you can do for them than in what you do, *so* be sure to spell out the value you create.

Careers

Here you can showcase any roles that are available within your company. While this feature is available in the free version of LinkedIn, you do have to pay a charge for it. For example, you can pay a fee of around £125.95 for a 30-day job posting: the fee will depend on location and reach.

Anyone can search jobs posts, while the paid-for versions of LinkedIn enable job seekers to filter further. However, if you post a job on the jobs board, anyone hitting the 'Jobs' tab and searching jobs will potentially have access to your post.

Services

Under Services you can include the range of services and products that you provide. You can create a stand-alone 'landing page' for each service you offer, ensuring that each service is leveraging relevant keywords and showcasing what you do. Not only can you add content on each page, you can also showcase videos relating to that specific product or service and also include a promotion.

Take a look at just one of the service pages from Hubspot's company page. It includes a keyword overview, recommendations, a video and

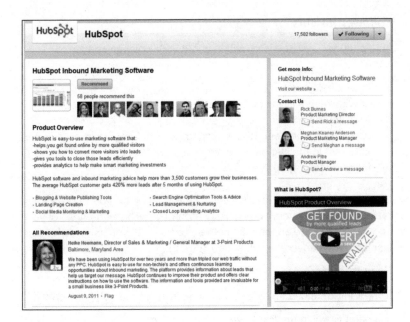

contact information. This information can be tailored differently on each specific product or service page, so that you can make your content highly targeted.

If you get this company profile right it can become another effective online presence for people who find you via LinkedIn. The steps are as follows.

1. Create a company profile.
2. Complete the profile with keyword-optimised and engaging content.
3. Encourage team members to create a personal profile and make connections.
4. Provide each team member with a standard 'boilerplate' which they can use when describing where they work.

Insights

Insights are analytical measurements that enable you to understand interactions.

These insights are broken down into three sections: follower insights; page insights; and employee insights.

Follower insights

In this tab you will see information about your company page:

- total followers
- recent followers
- new followers in the last seven days
- total impressions in the last seven days
- update engagement (those engaging with your company status updates) in the last seven days
- follower demographics.

You can see that there is a rich vein of information for you to keep track of. For example, if you focus activity around growing awareness of your company page and encouraging others to follow it, you can watch these insights and measure any changes in trends.

Page insights

Similar information can be gleaned on activity on the company profile:

- page views in the last seven days
- unique visitors in the last seven days
- page clicks in the last seven days
- page views (what visitors saw)
- page visitor demographics (owner, manager, entry, senior director, etc.)
- product and service page clicks (who's clicking what).

This data can be useful for measuring effort against impact. You can clearly see which pages are resonating.

Employee insights

This tab shows you which companies other people looked at when they were looking at 'Your Business'. 'People who looked at ABC also viewed . . .' This helps you to see who you are being aligned with and whether you have the right keywords in place.

'Departures' shows which employees have moved on and where they've moved to. This could be illuminating, providing useful insights into the competition.

Engaging your LinkedIn audience via a Poll

In the LinkedIn navigation, under the More tab, you'll see the option for Polls. Click this and you'll see that you can easily create a LinkedIn Poll. Polls provide a simple and effective way for you to engage with your audience and glean insight and feedback.

More ways to engage on LinkedIn...

Finding people via the company profile

'If you don't know the person you need to be speaking with – but you know the company they work for – then search company and check if you have any relevant connections.'

It may be that you know the person you want to connect with for business development opportunities. However, when you search for them on LinkedIn, there are no 1st, 2nd or 3rd degree connections – nor are they a member of any groups you are a member of – and so they show as 'Out of your Network'.

Before you give up on the connection – it's worth looking at their company profile, as it may be that someone else within their company is connected to you.

Effective lead generation via LinkedIn

From a business development perspective, LinkedIn provides a wonderful opportunity to seek out and target relevant connections. This simple three step process showcases how you can approach LinkedIn with business development in mind.

Given our mantra throughout this book is plan, listen, analyse before you engage, there's no surprise that we start with Step 1 – decide what you're setting out to achieve.

Step 1: Decide what you're setting out to achieve - is it that you are looking to:

- increase traffic to your site
- increase profile or company views
- increase email sign ups /downloads of guides/ebooks
- grow members to a LinkedIn Group
- increase in 1st degree connections
- convert connections to offline meetings

or a mix of these. Before you begin, decide what you want to achieve and ensure that the mechanisms are in place to enable your objectives.

Step 2: Build a target prospect profile

- What does the look like?
- Find them in Advanced Search (use the search fields such as company they work for, size, location, seniority etc.).
- Review/research their profiles.

Once you have your target prospect profile, you know exactly who you are looking for. For example, IT Managers within a 25 mile radius of Swindon could be the target. So you know exactly who you are looking for and can use Advanced Search to find them.

Step 3: Create a campaign

- Create emails/InMails or research people you know who will help you connect with your target. Then plan your activity, be it growing connections or making direct contact.
- Unless you plan for it to happen, it won't happen. Get the resources in place.

Of course, you will want to set some metrics so that you can measure how successful your activity is, and provided you have clear objectives at the outset – for example, to increase number of 1st degree connections – then you'll be able to measure how effective your efforts are.

LinkedIn Today

This is a really useful news service. It uses algorithms to match what your connections and you are talking about to deliver targeted news – in other words, it's an intelligent news feed. You see a snippet of the top articles on your home profile, and when you click on the LinkedIn Today link you're taken to your LinkedIn Today news page, where you can tailor even further the news you see. It also showcases top news sources and what's trending in your network.

Another useful feature is that you can 'save articles', creating a useful repository of business articles to keep, share and refer back to. It's definitely a feature worth using every day.

Finally: participate!

Try to look at your profile page every day. Every time you update your profile and show activity you are 'visible'. Remember: Visibility + Credibility = Profitability. In simple terms, the more visible you are to your contacts, the more they know about what you are up to, the more likely they are to contact you or think of you for a relevant reason, which may lead to business referral, hence profitability. Participation is key.

Social media marketing action plan

Clearly, LinkedIn is more than just a place to put your CV. As with all of the key social media networks, it is constantly evolving and tailoring its services.

In this chapter we showcased the many benefits of LinkedIn. To recap:

- It's a place to connect and reconnect.
- It can be used to connect the entire organisation.
- It's a useful Q&A resource.
- You can share information and expertise through Answers or through relevant groups.
- It's a database – you'll never lose your contacts.
- You can showcase who you are and what you do, and regularly update this information.
- You can showcase your organisation, and optimise products and service pages with keyword-optimised content, video and promotions.
- It's like Facebook for business.

---

8 | Listening and analysis

What you will learn from this chapter:

- Why listening is so important
- What you should be listening for
- Understanding your audience and influencers
- Techniques and tools for listening
- Analysis – taking those business insights and turning them into purposeful action

The importance of listening can't be underestimated. If someone is talking to you and you don't answer, at best you're unaware of the conversation – at worst, you're being ignorant.

You may have been told by a stern aunt or a schoolteacher, 'You've got two eyes, two ears and just one mouth – kindly use them in accordance.'

This statement also applies directly to all social media activity – listening is simply vital for marketing and communications strategies. Marketing itself has been defined as:

'fundamentally about understanding and anticipating the needs of the consumer so that organisations can create products and services to meet those needs, profitably.'

What's important to note are the two words **understanding** and **anticipating**. Both of these can be achieved only through effective listening and being close enough to consumers to understand and anticipate their needs.

In the past, listening would have focused on customer surveys, market research methods and consumer trends. Now we have social platforms where millions of people are sharing millions of conversations. This 'real-time' buzz and chatter is happening around the world 24/7 and across a range of social platforms. We live in an 'always on' society and with so much 'noise' being made across the social platforms, the challenge is to know how to cut through the noise to find the conversations that are relevant for you.

People to people

Listening is a very basic human function – it's one of the key senses that enable us to survive. And in business, listening aids survival too.

Think about listening from a people-to-people perspective and take the art of listening into the real networking world for a moment. Let's say you meet someone at a networking event. You walk up to them and, before you even ask their name, or what they do, or why they are here and how they're finding the event, you start talking at them. You don't let them get a word in, you just keep talking. If they ask a question, you ignore it and carry on talking and sharing your news. At best, they'll smile before they walk away, thinking you're a conceited egomaniac!

Listening is one part of conversing. If social networking is about continuous conversations, you can't just shout at your audience all the time. To strike an effective balance, you need to be continuously listening too. When we talk about focused listening versus unfocused publishing, we mean that if you have listened to customer need, you will be prepared to publish meaningful content. Instead of simply sharing what you think your customers want to hear, listen in and find out what matters to them. Then create content and solutions based around that need.

Social story

A technical devices company was very keen to create regular videos as part of their content mix. Because they often had to create product demonstrations they already had in-house resources which they could use to create video on an ongoing basis.

They set about creating a suite of videos, all based on things they thought would be useful to their audience. While the videos were very well put together, the level of engagement from their customers was disappointing. That's when they reached out for some advice.

They were encouraged to do some focused listening as to what was happening in their space, reviewing what their competitors were doing, looking at feedback on customer forums and listening in to real-time conversations on both Facebook and Twitter.

What they discovered was that there were a number of clear 'pain points' around a couple of the products. Recurring themes related to upgrade features and practical elements such as transferring data from one device to another. Armed with this information, the company created a suite of videos that focused on those very challenges.

Focused listening resulted in creating content which was highly engaging – not only for their customers, but for others having similar issues with competitor services using the same devices. The traction to the videos was significant and far surpassed their usual web traffic levels.

This confirms that in many cases, it's powerful to respond to a shared need rather than pushing out content that isn't targeted. Targeted content really does show who's been listening.

If you listen to the challenges of your audiences and potential audiences, you will be able to provide solutions. You can then target those solutions direct to the people asking questions or looking for solutions. And of course, if a few vocal people have an issue around a particular area, it's likely that you are also meeting the needs of those quieter, less vocal audiences too.

What should you be listening for?

Depending on what you are listening for (which should relate back to your objectives), the listening may take hours, days, weeks or even months – but it needs to happen. Listening in helps you to gain some really useful insights:

- what's important to the people you want to connect with
- what's being said in your sector
- what the influencers are talking about
- when they are visible
- what they are looking for
- what problems or challenges they have
- what solutions they are looking for
- what your competitors are talking about
- what people are engaging with
- when they are engaging
- what's working
- what the issues are
- what they are saying about you, your brand, your products.

Listening is so important that a whole new industry has been created around it. A growing number of marketing agencies, social media agencies, advertising agencies, as well as PR agencies, now offer 'social listening' services. Simply type the words 'social media listening' into Google and you'll find a huge and growing number of tools and services, some of which we have mentioned in this book.

Uncovering insights

When you listen (which is effectively like real-time research), you want to make sure that you are actively learning in order to glean useful insights to increase your knowledge about your market and audiences. Applying the tried and tested fact-finding questions – who, what, why, when, where – can provide some valuable insights, as the box below shows.

Who?

- Who are they?
- What is their demographic profile?

Discover if their gender, age, location aligns with your typical customer profile.

What?

- What did they engage with?
- What did they share and with whom?

Learn about what's working and create more targeted content to drive engagement.

When?

- At what time of day are they engaging?
- On mobile/desktop/tablets?

Understand how times of engagement (weekends, weekdays, working hours, out-of-hours) influence platforms used, and vice versa.

Where?

- Where did they come from? Twitter, Facebook, LinkedIn, Google+, YouTube, blog?
- What's driving them to your site?
- Which platforms are they on?
- Can you see any patterns?

You can start to build a picture of which channels your audiences are using, and what's driving what.

> **Why?**
>
> - Why are they engaging?
> - What made them engage?
>
> Understanding this gives you ideas for improving engagement tactics, such as offers, free guides, downloads, referrals from other sites.

Business intelligence

Data is one thing, but interpreting it is another. The who, what, when, where and why example box demonstrates that even with basic analysis you can glean a significant amount of information. What's important is that the information is then turned into business insights which help to drive strategy and tactics.

Tune in to your influencers

Just as Pareto analysis delivers the 80/20 rule – 20% of customers deliver 80% of profits – there is similar analysis at play in social media and online. In 2012, Meteor Solutions collected data from more than 20 brand marketer clients. Their research identified that on average, approximately 1% of a site's audience generated 20% of all its traffic, through sharing the brand's content or sharing site links with others. These influencers are clearly key to amplification and it was shown that their influence also drove a higher share of conversion.

Once you have identified who your influencers are, it is clear that there will be benefits from developing relationships with them. Directly engaging with them and sharing exclusive opportunities, special offers – perhaps even unique content – will be beneficial, as these influencers will be far more powerful in creating a buzz than you are.

Of course, the challenge is to befriend these influencers in a very human way. Using social media isn't about direct selling, as we've said throughout this book, it's about getting people to know you, like you, trust you – building share of mind so that they ultimately do business with you. If you focus attention on 'pushing' sales messages at these valuable influencers, you run the risk of being too promotional – and losing your biggest fans.

Advocacy is probably the most powerful form of promotion. Once you've found your influencers, develop a programme (strategy/tactics) to nurture and develop this valuable channel in the most authentic and engaging way possible. The more raving fans you can create for your business, the more advocates you will have out there in the market place amplifying your marketing for you. If people are saying great things about you, your products, your services – and sharing links and information – you need to know who they are, thank them, get to know them and build relationships to keep them happy and busy.

Listening for relevant conversations

A great way to start listening to what's being said is to track relevant keywords. Even without a formal social media dashboard (see Chapter 9) in place, you can track important keywords online and set alerts, so that you are notified of any mentions as they happen. Google Alerts and Social Mention are very useful, but there is a range of other services such as TweetBeep or Twilert.

Google Alerts

A simple tool like Google Alerts (www.google.com/alerts) will enable you to track what is being said about your brand, services or products. You can set alerts about absolutely anything, and whenever those words are mentioned online, you will receive an alert. You might, for example, want to track competitors or a key influencer.

Google Alerts sweep content that has been indexed by Google. Tweets and Facebook updates get into these alerts too. You can decide when to receive your alerts: you can have them sent to you in real time as they happen, once a day or once a week.

Social Mention

This service is similar to Google Alerts but specifically designed for the social networks. You can choose what you wish to track – for example your name, brand or product mentions (on Twitter, Facebook, YouTube and other social platforms) – and again, you can set the frequency with which you receive alerts. If you are using a social dashboard you will also have options to track keywords and sentiment.

Whichever platform you choose to use, you need to be clear about what you are tracking and why. There are a number of ways of tracking keywords and key phrases:

1. **Finding new followers:** Let's say you want to follow people who are talking and sharing about social media, professional services marketing and user experience. You can track these keywords to help you tune in to relevant conversations.
2. **Tracking competitor activity:** Watching what's happening in their 'keyword' space and being alerted to any relevant followers, influencers and conversations.

3. **Brand reputation:** Tracking your own brand/product names.
4. **Tracking direct response key phrases.** By this we mean key phrases that not only house the keyword but also include a direct response element such as 'looking for help with'/'can anyone help with'. You can string these key phrases together with keywords to help target relevant conversations. This is quite useful when leveraging social platforms for lead generation.

As always, you should be very clear about what you are looking to achieve – this will determine what you look out for.

Other useful tools to help you see conversations, who is saying what and influencer reach include the following applications (we've already mentioned some of these in previous chapters):

- Klout (www.klout.com)
- Kred (www.kred.com)
- Peer Index (www.peerindex.com)
- Sprout Social (www.sproutsocial.com)
- The Archivist (www.thearchivist.com)
- Tweetreach (www.tweetreach.com)
- TwentyFeet (www.twentyfeet.com)
- Twitcleaner (www.twitcleaner.com)
- Twitonomy (twitonomy.com).

These applications (and others) enable you to track engagement and sentiment, and view influencer reach, but if you are focusing on specific objectives, you may prefer to determine your own set of analysis criteria to monitor and measure.

Some areas you might wish to include in your analysis criteria are:

- members and number of active profiles
- posts – frequency and density
- comments and brand mentions (including sentiment – positive or negative)
- inbound links/traffic
- tags, votes, bookmarks.

And for value awareness and influence:

- brand loyalty/affinity
- media placements
- share of conversation
- sentiment of posts
- interaction with content.

Determining your objectives is key to understanding what you need to be listening for. However, not only do you need to be clear about what signals you need to listen out for, you should ideally keep listening in a continuous and concerted way. Conversations on social media are continuous, so you need to develop processes and systems for listening and learning in a continuous way too.

Plan to listen: developing a social media listening strategy

Let's take a step-by-step look at a simple, practical approach.

1 Determine where your audience is

Once you start listening you will very quickly start to gauge which platforms your audiences are participating in. For example, if you are a professional services firm, you'll be listening out for who is talking about what on which platform:

- Are people talking about 'professional services' on Twitter, Facebook, LinkedIn or Google+?
- What type of people are talking about your sector?
- Are there any influencers who stand out and that you need to be connecting with?

Listening in is illuminating. Listen often and regularly, then analyse who is talking. You will quickly build up a pattern and learn which platforms are 'noisier' and what part each social network plays in your sector. Use the what, when, who, where, when model to build metrics that help you learn about your audience.

2 Identify your influencers

Listening in is key to understanding who the influencers are in your space. Influencers can be highly valuable to a business. The more you understand who they are, the easier it will be to find more of them. The more influencers you have, the more reach and amplification opportunity you create.

Watch who is sharing your information, sharing links and driving audiences to find out about you. Many of the services we've mentioned in this chapter (particularly Kred and Peer Index) provide you with analytics about just how influential your influencers' sharing activity is. Know your influencers – perhaps categorise them as A, B, C and D – and build a programme to nurture your As and Bs as well as moving your Cs and Ds to As and Bs.

3 Understand the data

In many ways, this is an age of data overload. There are so many facts and figures available, it can be a struggle to make sense of the chaos of information you receive. It may initially seem a daunting task, but it's worth understanding what the data is telling you. Data speaks and you need to create a process to help you mine the gems you need out of the mass of information. You could use customer demographics, purchase patterns, online transactions driven by social interaction – you decide. Once you understand the metrics that are important for your business, you can listen more insightfully to the wealth of data available via social media networks.

4 Know your keywords

To tune in to relevant conversations, you need to start somewhere. This is where keywords are useful – you can start to listen in to the words that are relevant to your business and track conversations in real time. We explained keywords in some detail in Chapter 3. As we said, keywords are the DNA of your online visibility, so be sure you know what yours are. Track conversations around those keywords, set alerts in Google Alerts and Social Mention, or in your social dashboard (see Chapter 9), so that you are informed and can build insights around keywords that matter to your business.

5 Create listening criteria

Even when you're using targeted resources to help you tailor your 'social listening' effectively, because conversation is continuous there's an awful lot to listen out for. So set yourself some robust listening criteria based on what is relevant for your business and your specific objectives. Your criteria might include:

- how many times you were mentioned
- sentiment – positive or negative
- by which audience
- on which platform
- in what context.

And, of course, while we've focused primarily on gleaning information from the social networks don't forget that you may also be able to gather rich information from industry forums or specialist blogs. Be mindful that your 'listening' might need to extend beyond what's happening on social networks. This is why it's often good to include a blend of automated listening tools such as Google Alerts and Social Mention. While the latter focuses on social networks, Google Alerts will pick up 'online' activity generally.

We've explored a number of platforms that enable you to use your eyes and ears online, but whichever platforms you decide to choose, and even if you choose not to participate on any of the social platforms, you can still be listening and gleaning insights from all the chatter that's happening online.

The key message is – to be informed, be sure you're listening.

> ## Social media marketing action plan
>
> - Measurement and analysis aids continuous learning.
> - Create listening criteria that are relevant to your objectives.
> - Explore the tools for listening and choose the right one(s) for you.
> - Identify your influencers and build a programme to nurture them and grow more of them.
> - Determine the who, what, when, where and why of your audience.
> - Plan to listen.

9 | Daily management of social media

What you will learn from this chapter:

- The range of multiple account management platforms
- Set-up and daily management via HootSuite
- Creating streams of information
- Scheduling
- Shrinking links
- Measurement of social media marketing activity

You will be aware by now that embracing social media platforms requires a significant commitment.

Often, when we're training or consulting, people realise the magnitude of what the channels offer and ask the question, '*Is there a simple way to manage multiple accounts?*' Fortunately, the answer to that question is a very loud **yes**. Welcome to social media dashboards.

Social platform dashboards have been around for as long as many of the social networks, so it's staggering to find out that roughly 80% of the businesses and practitioners we train (some with very established social media presences) do not use or are unaware of social media dashboards. This means that many people managing business Twitter, Facebook or LinkedIn accounts are literally logging in and out of each separate social media network each time they want to share an update. For example, the basic Twitter platform, while it's been enhanced significantly over the years to make it far more user friendly, still has its limitations. For example, let's say we wanted to schedule a tweet for tomorrow, an hour from now, next week or next month. Unless you are using a complementary application (e.g. Buffer, which sits within Twitter. com – refer back to Chapter 4) you can't do this on Twitter. As soon as you set up the tweet you have to send it.

Social dashboards

There are various social media dashboards. Some of them are totally free to use while others offer a free starter service with enterprise versions. Just a few of the many are Tweetdeck, Sprout Social (free trial option), CoTweet, Social Oomph and NetVibes. Then there are more advanced enterprise-only solutions such as Radian6 (now part of Sales Force Marketing Cloud), Meltwater and Sysomos in which the dashboard is specifically tailored as a management, listening and reporting platform. (Note: many of the free versions also have sophisticated enterprise versions – the enterprise versions we mention here don't have free versions.)

Both of us have experimented with Tweetdeck, Twhirl, CoTweet and we've had dealings with Radian6, but the one we both favour and have stuck with throughout our personal Twitter journeys has been HootSuite.

In this chapter we'll showcase the workings of HootSuite as a social media dashboard, but there are many other social measurement, monitoring and listening tools to automate activity. It's entirely up to you to decide which one best fits your tastes and needs.

HootSuite

This book is concerned with the practical side of social media, so we thought it only right to showcase the platform that we believe to be the most practical and user friendly. HootSuite (www.hootsuite.com) has various levels of enterprise solutions – from very basic to more sophisticated options – but the free version is a great starting point to get to grips with what you can expect from a social media dashboard.

In this chapter we'll look at setting up your account and scheduling communications. We'll also touch on listening in and managing social conversations.

Getting started

Step 1: Setting up your account

Hoo's Using HootSuite

Visit www.hootsuite.com and set up your account. This is really very simple – you need a username and unique email address for each account, and that's pretty much it.

Step 2: Bringing in your social network accounts

Connecting the dashboard with any social networks you have already created is, again, relatively simple. On the left-hand side of the dashboard you'll see a range of icons. The first is the Owl icon. When you click on the Owl you will see an account overview. In the area 'My Social Networks' the various social networks you are already streaming into the dashboard are outlined. You can add new social network accounts into the stream via 'Add a Social Network'.

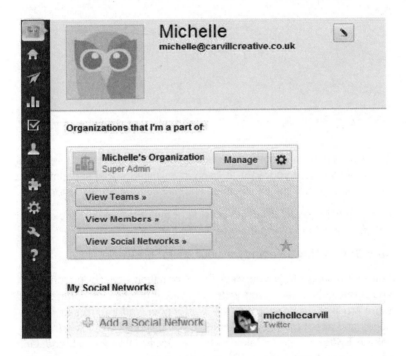

When you click the 'Add a Social Network' box, you are presented with a menu asking which social network you wish to pull through to the dashboard. Select the medium (Twitter, Facebook, LinkedIn, etc.) and verify your username, email address and password for the account you wish to pull through.

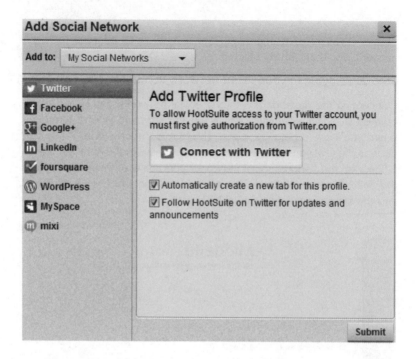

The free version of HootSuite enables you to bring in up to five social media accounts. If you want to bring in unlimited social accounts, you will have to opt for the Pro Version and pay a fee of $9.99 a month.

Should you have requirements outside of their Free or Pro version, you can tailor a solution. And that steps into Enterprise territory.

Step 3: Creating streams for your social network

You can manage how you view the information coming in from each social media account. Even with the many changes and updates (and there are likely to be more) to the Twitter.com platform, to see @ messages and direct messages plus lists, you still have to click on various links in Twitter.com to be taken to those specific information feeds. One of the major assets of HootSuite (and indeed other platforms) is that all the information that is usually hidden behind tabs and links within Twitter.com can be laid out in a 'single view' social media dashboard.

And, of course, you can manage the order of the information feeds, giving you control over how that 'single view' dashboard is arranged.

You can see from the image below that we have arranged the @michellecarvill Twitter account as Home Feed, then for this demo we've created a stream for our training hashtag, #smetraining2012 (now 2013), then @Mentions, then Sent Tweets and so on. You can have up to 10 streams in any one account.

The image below shows that you have the option to bring in streams around:

- Home Feed
- Mentions
- Direct Message (Inbox and Outbox)
- Sent Tweets
- Favourite Tweets
- Retweets to me
- Retweets by me
- My Tweets, Retweeted
- Scheduled Tweets.

This will give you a considerable amount of information that you can choose keep your eye on.

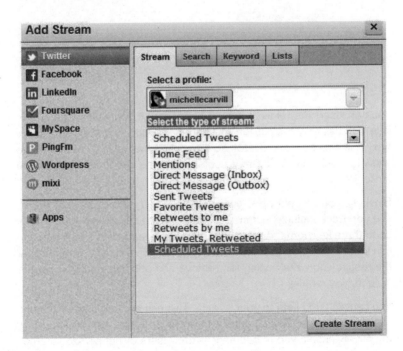

There are also tabs for **Search**, **Keyword** and **Lists**. And this is where HootSuite can become really useful for centralising your 'social listening'. For example, let's say you want to **search** on the noise going on around a certain hashtag or some other keywords. It could be a company name – Carvill Creative – or a person's name – Michelle Carvill – or a keyword/phrase that's relevant to you, e.g. 'social media training'.

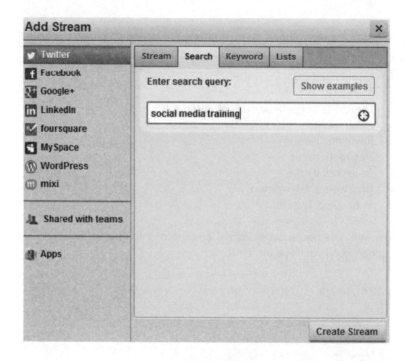

You can insert the relevant search query and, if you want, click on the little compass-style circle on the right-hand side of the search query box. This acts as a geolocator, so that only 'local' search results will be shown, which makes it really useful in cutting out irrelevant location noise.

Similarly, you can set up **keywords**. While you can't geolocate these, you can track multiple instances. The Keyword tab allows you to track up to three keywords. Adding and removing keywords is simple, so you can test results very quickly. If the keywords you are using don't deliver the results you were hoping for, remove and optimise until you get the insights you require.

You can also add **lists** to your stream. This can be really useful in monitoring List activity. (See Chapter 4 for more on Twitter lists.) Twitter lists effectively enable you to segment Twitter users or put people, such as your competitors, into lists, so that you can watch conversations without having to follow them. You can see on the opposite page that you

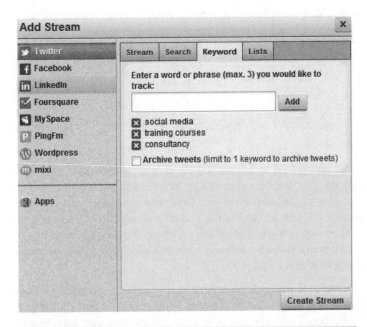

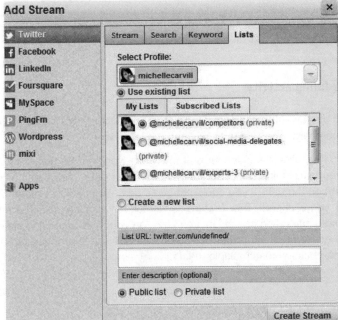

simply select your profile, select the relevant list and then create a stream – *et voilà*, the list will appear as a stream of data on your dashboard. You can then watch what's going on in that list, alongside your social media management.

In HootSuite you also have the option to create a new list, so you can create lists via this platform too.

Step 4: Using HootSuite to schedule your social media activity

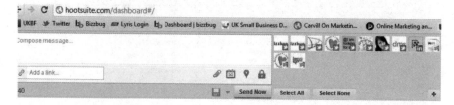

On your dashboard is a mechanism to share information directly via HootSuite. To compose a message, simply click the top left-hand corner of your dashboard. Click on 'Compose message' and write your message. You can add a URL link and/or an image and then over on the right-hand side of the message box you'll see the range of accounts that you have pulled through, so you can select which accounts are relevant to share that 'message' from.

For example, if you want to send the message to the Michelle Carvill Twitter account, the Carvill Creative Twitter account and post it to the Michelle Carvill LinkedIn Profile too (should the message be relevant to hit all three networks), you can simply create one message and send it to all three networks simply by checking the boxes showing these accounts.

Scheduling activity

If you don't want to send your messages immediately, you can schedule any number of messages to be sent at a later date.

To do this, click the calendar button (which works in the same way as conventional online calendars) and choose your date. There are no limitations on the date – you could schedule something weeks, months or even years ahead! This feature is useful for aligning social activity around a marketing campaign: you can plan your messages and schedule them to fit in with other activities so that there is a concerted and planned push across multiple media.

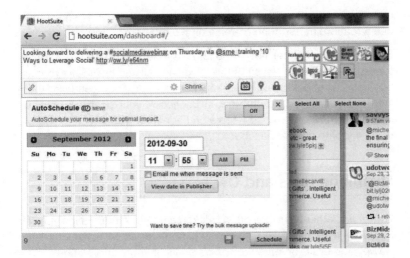

Once activity is scheduled, you can review and, if relevant, approve any pending messages. So any typos or any messages that are irrelevant can easily be amended, rescheduled or removed.

If you are using the Enterprise Version – and have a number of team members all using the same platform – it may be that someone needs to approve the messages before they are deployed. And HootSuite offers a 'Require Approval' feature too.

You'll also see the AutoSchedule feature. This feature is relatively new to HootSuite (launched August 2012). If you switch this feature to On, HootSuite will endeavour to determine the optimum time to send your messages. This is based on historical activity of the account and when people are sharing and connecting with you.

The other great feature is that if you schedule to send one message to numerous accounts, the AutoSchedule feature will automatically stagger the messages, so that your message doesn't hit all accounts/networks at the same time.

Sharing updates to LinkedIn or Facebook via HootSuite

When sharing an update to either Facebook or LinkedIn via HootSuite, you still get to say a bit more. These platforms don't have the same 140-character restrictions as Twitter and you'll notice that when you make an update and include LinkedIn or Facebook accounts you still get to say more.

Our advice is always to be as targeted as possible to each audience. People on your Facebook Page will expect a certain dialogue, Twitter is much faster and more fluid, while it's worth remembering that your

LinkedIn connections are mainly your professional network, so you may use a totally different tone of voice on that platform.

So do be mindful that not all updates will be appropriate for all platforms: one message doesn't fit all. You can still use HootSuite to manage your Facebook posts or LinkedIn updates, but you can tailor them individually. Also be mindful that in Facebook your post will show as coming from HootSuite, so people on Facebook will know that you are using a tool to post to Facebook.

Shrinking links and Ow.ly

Twitter and other platforms often limit the amount of information you can include in a status update. Twitter is famous for its 140-character limit. However, there is an easy way of cramming in more information.

For example, let's say you want to include a link to a blog post or article you have found. This is the link: http://www.carvillcreative.co.uk/blog/how-to-watch-your-competitors-on-twitter-without-them-knowing/. It comes in at a whopping 100 characters, not leaving you with very much space to add a compelling headline or your viewpoint. If you paste that link into the link box and hit 'shrink' (all automated for you via Hoot-Suite), the 100-character link is shortened to just 18 characters: http://ow.ly/e64Km.

There are other URL shrinking tools such as www.bitly.com and http://tinyurl.com, but these are stand-alone websites that aren't built into dashboards, as HootSuite is.

Understanding your social media account activity

Measuring activity around your social media accounts is important and can provide some interesting insights. For example, the content that people are engaging with, which posts are getting shared the most, etc. HootSuite has an Analytics tab – some report services are free while some are paid for.

For example, as we've just discussed the Ow.ly URL shortener, you can see that there are reports which you can review via HootSuite. These reports provide you with information around your activity. You can set date ranges and which profile

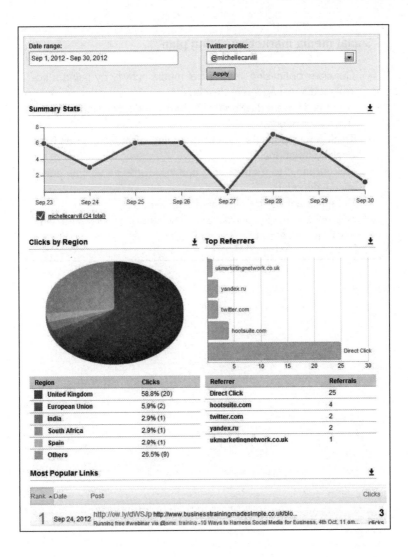

you wish to review, and then you will be able to see a host of information.

There are standard reports and there are report templates that you can tailor, enabling you to craft reports that will give you the analytics that matter for your business. You can also bring in other analytics to keep all your data in one centralised dashboard. Google Analytics can be brought into HootSuite, as can Facebook Insights.

Social media marketing action plan

- Consider optimising your social media activity by using a social media management dashboard.
- Test the different dashboard platforms and see which one best suits your needs.
- Think about both the practical sharing of messages and the analytic functions.
- Use streams to monitor lists and keywords as well as social media accounts.
- Schedule activity for maximum effectiveness.
- Set up some key performance indicators to measure your social media activity.

10 | Understanding and using other social media sites

> What you will learn from this chapter:
>
> - Background to the other key social networks
> - Understanding their relevance to your business
> - How to build them into your marketing strategy
> - Introduction to Google+, Pinterest, Flickr, Tumblr, MySpace and Foursquare
> - Setting up profiles

Throughout this book, we have focused on the four key social networks: Facebook, Twitter, YouTube and LinkedIn. However, there are hundreds of other online sites where people can communicate, interact and network.

These sites cover a wide range of interests. From disabilities (www.disaboom.com) to clubbing (www.dontstayin.com) and from environmental issues (www.wiser.org) to African communities (www.lagbook.com), there are literally hundreds of sites that incorporate social networking.

It is also worth noting that while the 'Big Four' may be huge across much of the globe, in some parts of the world they are eclipsed by local sites. In China, there are home-grown versions of Facebook (Renren – www.renren.com), Twitter (Sina Weibo – www.weibo.com) and YouTube (Youku – www.youku.com) as well as Tencent (www.tencent.com), Douban (www.douban.com) and the mobile app Wechat. In Brazil, the Google-owned site Orkut (www.orkut.com) is very popular, while in Norway Biip, with 430,000 users, is the second most popular site after Facebook.

For internal networking Yammer (www.yammer.com) and Chatter (www.chatter.com) are proving to be very effective tools for breaking down silos within organisations and improving employee engagement.

It is also worth mentioning MySpace, once *the* social network, which has seen its fortunes rise and fall and rise again over the last few years. Launched in 2003, it was the most popular social networking site between 2005 and 2008, becoming well used by artists and musicians. It notably kick-started the career of the singer Lily Allen. Now owned by

Justin Timberlake, it has seen something of a renaissance in recent times and now has 25 million users (as of June 2012).

The one thing all these sites have in common is **user-generated content**. They are also all available as mobile apps – which is important when you consider that in many parts of the world people do have smartphones but do not have access to broadband or even landlines.

Most of these sites operate on similar platforms. There is a main news feed area which is tailored by the user, a list of suggested friends/contacts/pages/sites, a section where you can post your own content and a menu listing services.

When to use these sites

As we have emphasised throughout this book, it is important to focus on both your own business objectives and your target audiences. If you are a European company looking to increase your brand profile in China, it would be worth investing in a decent Renren page for your brand. Similarly, if you are looking to market your product to an Indian audience, it might be better to use Bharatstudent (www.bharatstudent.com), one of the most popular social networking sites in India, than Facebook.

Using the Plan, Listen, Analyse and Engage mantra, it is useful to ascertain exactly who your target audiences are, what channels they are using and how best to engage with them. As with all aspects of marketing, this process needs to be done constantly, as social networks gain or lose popularity and users change their media consumption habits.

Using data from a site like Alexa (www.alexa.com), it is possible to get traffic data, global rankings and other information on thousands of websites, including the key social networking sites.

The two key questions you should always ask yourself are: 'Will having a presence on this site benefit my business?' and 'Will the return on investment be worth the effort?' Unfortunately, many brands have signed up to a plethora of sites as eagerly as dictators collect phoney medals. While there may be some short-term PR value associated with being on seven or eight social media sites, there is unlikely to be much benefit in the medium or long term. In fact, if most of the sites are just 'there for show', it may even harm your brand.

It is important to understand that whatever site you choose to use, you should incorporate it into your overall marketing strategy. As with Facebook and Twitter, you need to look at your tone of voice, understand your keywords, post the right content and listen to the conversations taking place.

And you will need to monitor effectiveness against the KPIs that you will have set when setting up the sites. If a particular social network is not working for you, there will be two possible explanations: either you're not using it effectively or it is not the correct marketing channel for you.

A final note: virtually all social networking sites integrate with each other, thereby making it easy to share information across a range of different mediums and audiences. But don't just scattergun your content across everything. You need to think about the specific audience for each social networking site.

Google+

Launched in June 2011, Google+ was Google's latest foray into social networking after Google Buzz and Google Friend Connect. In just over six months, the platform amassed more than 90 million users and now has more than 400 million users. As a business, Google is always looking at ways to make more money, so Google+ was set up as a way to help them become a better search engine by capturing more information and real-time conversations.

Integrated into the suite of services offered by Google – Gmail, maps, analytics, YouTube, Documents, Calendar – Google+ was initially focused on individual users, but in November 2011, Google rolled out business pages in the same way that Facebook did.

Google+ allows people and businesses to create pages and develop relationships with prospects and customers on multiple levels. Individuals can add a brand to a specific Google+ circle, share a Google+ page with their network, and interact with the content posted by that company.

The key benefit of using Google+ as part of your overall marketing strategy is not linked to social networking per se. By posting dynamic, keyword-rich and engaging content on the site, in conjunction with an overall search engine optimisation strategy, a company or brand will be rewarded by having a higher visibility on Google than they would if they posted content in a blog or on other social networking sites.

Just before the launch of Google+, Google had an agreement with Twitter to include their updates in their search results through a special feed. Updates to Facebook Pages were also included in their search results. However, with this 'fire hose' now switched off, results on Google+ are now ranked more highly than those on Facebook or Twitter.

So, if one of your strategic business objectives is to have a higher visibility on Google, it may be that Google+ would be well worth investigating.

Setting up a business page on Google+

As Google+ is part of the suite of Google applications, the first step is to set up an accessible Gmail account for your organisation. Ideally this should be an account that is accessible to multiple members of your marketing or management team, e.g. companymarketingteam@gmail. com. If you already have a YouTube account, you will be able to sign in using the same Gmail address.

Once you have set up or signed into Google, visit https://plus.google. com/pages/create to create your page. In much the same way as on Facebook, you can choose which category you wish your page to appear in. Simply fill in the form, agree to the Google+ terms and your page will have been created. Now you need to customise your profile with a decent profile image (252 × 252 pixels), details about your web-site or landing page (if applicable) and a 10-word strapline that describes your product or service.

At this stage you need to consider who the administrators for your page will be. According to Google+, '*Each page can only have one owner, but can have up to 50 managers*' (see http://bit.ly/Rttogh for more details). These people can be invited via email.

Once the page has been created you need to customise it with content. This includes a cover image (940 × 180 pixels), a boilerplate about your organisation (similar to that on Facebook or Twitter), some decent images and, if applicable, videos, events and links.

Creating content

When your page is complete, you can start posting content. This can be done in two ways. First, you can access Google+ via either your PC or mobile device and fill in the 'Share What's New' box with an article, photo, video or link. If you have a company blog or news feed, it's a great idea to post these to your Google+ Page. Remember to use a keyword-rich title plus a web link to the post on your blog or website. This will help improve your visibility on Google as well as widening the audience for your posts. As with Facebook, the more interesting and engaging content you post, the more likely it is that people will see it and the higher your visibility will be.

The second way to add content is to click the +1 that you see listed on websites or next to news articles. This will automatically share the con-tent on your page's wall.

Building a community on Google+

The Google+ community is made up of circles (www.google.com/ Circles). These are networks of people or organisations who you can categorise in much the same way as you create lists on Twitter or lists of friends on Facebook.

By organising your network into these separate folders, you can target who you wish to communicate with. For example, if you were an organic farm shop, you could have circles for your suppliers, vegetarian customers and those who eat meat. Doing this means that when you are updating your site with content, you will target the correct audience rather than just sending a blanket mailout.

In a similar way to LinkedIn, where you have a three-tier set of contacts, on Google+ you have extended circles. Here, you have the option to promote your content to those people or organisations in your Circles' Circles.

Here are some ways of increasing your network on Google+.

1. Add a +1 Button to your website.
2. Post regular content – ideally at least once a day.
3. Look for people and organisations in the search bar and put them into one of your circles.
4. Use the 'Ripples' function, which helps you to find new and interesting people or organisations to follow based on who has been sharing information posted on Google+. (More at http://support.google.com/plus/bin/answer.py?hl=en&answer=1713320.)

Pinterest

The newest kid on the social media block is Pinterest. Launched in March 2010 on an invitation-only basis, the site opened up fully in August 2012. Based on the idea of pinning content to virtual pinboards, Pinterest saw phenomenal growth of 4377% between May 2011 and May 2012 (www.comscore.com) and by July 2012 had over 20 million global users. Quickly adopted by women, the site is also seeing strong growth from brands eager to make use of the visual interface.

On Pinterest, users can share, curate and discover new interests by posting (or 'pinning') content such as images or videos on their own or others' 'pinboards' – online noticeboards. This content can come from a variety of sources such as their PC, smartphone, via a 'Pin It' button on a website or a URL.

Who can use Pinterest?

Pinterest is a very visual medium which lends itself very easily to creative industries such as art, design, architecture, photography, etc. Pinboards can act as online mood boards illustrating the thought processes of the artists or designers, reflecting their influences and showing the creative journey.

However, there are a wide variety of organisations who could use Pinterest to fulfil business objectives such as brand awareness, product promotion or lead generation.

Case study: ASOS

Online department store ASOS (www.pinterest.com/asos) are successfully using the site for product and lifestyle ideas, celebrity content and competitions. They have 19 different boards, 1,251 pins and almost 13,000 followers.

Rather than simply using Pinterest as a sales tool – which is discouraged and never a good idea on social media anyway – the brand is pinning ideas and giving an insight into what fashions and styles they like.

Setting up a profile

It's simplest to get started on Pinterest if you already have an existing corporate Twitter account. Simply sign into your account, then go to www.pinterest.com and sign up by clicking on the 'Connect with Twitter' button.

Alternatively, you can sign up using your email address. As with other social networks, it is advisable to select a generic corporate email address such as pinterest@mycompany.co.uk and ensure that the password is stored safely. This means that there will still be control over the site should you, or the other administrator(s), move on.

Once the account has been set up, you will need to select your company or brand name as your username, then complete your profile information including description and logo plus a link to your website or applicable landing page. Once this is done, you are ready to go.

Pinning and attracting a following on Pinterest

As with a Facebook Page, before trying to build a following, you need some content. In the case of Pinterest it is worth creating your own pinboards. For example, if you are a photographer and you specialise in weddings, corporate shots and events, you could create different pinboards for each category – much as you would create landing pages on a website. Alternatively, if you are an estate agent with a number of different offices, you could create pinboards to reflect the areas where you sell properties.

To create a board, click on the Add button and scroll down to 'Create a Board'. You will have the opportunity to choose a board name and category. There is also the option to invite other pinners to post on the board – much as you would invite someone to be a guest blogger.

How to pin

There are several ways of finding material to pin to your board. The simplest is via websites with a 'Pin It' button next to articles. This will automatically add the material to whichever pinboard you select.

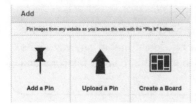

Alternatively, when you find something of interest on a web page, copy the URL, go into Pinterest and click on the Add button. Click on Add a Pin, copy the link and hit Find Images. It will then pin it to your board.

The third way is to upload content directly from your own PC or mobile device. Again, click on the Add a Pin button but this time select Upload a Pin.

Note: As with publishing anything online or offline, it is important that you have the permission of the author/creator or you run the risk of copyright infringement.

What to pin

Just as you aim to fill a Facebook Page with interesting and engaging content, the same is true on Pinterest. Imagine each pinboard as being like a blank canvas that you have to turn into a piece of art which will be exhibited in a museum frequented by your target audience as well as the general public.

As with any form of content creation, it is important to have a strategy. Who is your target audience, what objective are you trying to meet and how will it add value to your brand?

Case study

You are an architect and want to showcase not only the buildings you have designed but also the designers and architects who have influenced you the most. You could create a board entitled 'My Designs' where you would upload images and links to your own work. At the same time, you could create another board entitled 'My Influences' and pin images from other websites. You may even decide to create a board entitled 'Great Architects', which would highlight your contemporaries and their designs.

> An excellent example of this is Emu Architects in Reggio Emilia, Italy (http://pinterest.com/emuarchitects). Their pinboards reflect the work they do, their influences and designs they like in a way that a website never could.

Pinterest is a very visual medium, so you should ensure that the URLs you post or the images you upload are of a high enough quality and will look good on your board.

Sharing through social media

As with blogs and videos, it is important to have a campaign in place for promoting both your boards and your pins. Pinterest and Facebook are natural bedfellows and there is a button to Like content and post it to a Facebook profile.

At the same time, you can use your other social networks – Twitter, LinkedIn and Google+ – to promote your Pinterest page and publicise it on other marketing channels.

Finally, remember that Pinterest is a network. Try to Like as many other applicable Pinterest users to build your network and show that you are part of a community.

Ways to use Pinterest for your business

- **Thought leadership:** Show that you are a person of influence in your sector by showcasing your thoughts and influences.
- **Events:** Pinterest is a great way to add colour to an event you hosted or attended.
- **Video:** As well as images, you can also pin videos, which can add an extra dimension to your boards.
- **Humanising your brand:** You could create a board for your staff to illustrate the human side of your organisation.
- **Social search:** By using hashtags in the same way as on Twitter, you can tag specific keywords, which will ensure that you stay visible online.

Flickr

If YouTube has become the pre-eminent video file-sharing site, Flickr (www.flickr.com) is the leader in photo file-sharing. Started in 2004 and bought by Yahoo! in 2005, this site has become one of the most popular ways to display and categorise images. Only the Facebook-owned

flickr
Home
You
Organize & Create
Contacts
Groups
Explore
Upload
Help
Upgrade
Sign Out
Search
Search
Photos
Groups
People
Everyone's Uploads
calverts
SEARCH
Full Text
Tags Only
Advanced Search
Sort:
Relevant
Recent
Interesting
View:
Small
Medium
Detail
Slideshow

Instagram (www.instagram.com) comes close to it in terms of functionality and popularity.

There are two types of account – one free and one paid for. The free account allows users up to 300Mb of images plus the ability to showcase up to 200 photos and two videos. With the paid-for version you get unlimited uploads, unlimited viewing of your photo library, the opportunity to upload and play unlimited HD videos and access to statistics on your account.

On the site, images take centre stage and can be grouped, arranged, discussed and used as the basis for conversations. As with all social networking channels though, it is **not** a place to sell your products directly but a way to initiate conversation with your customers or target audiences. Initially, and for a long time, Flickr was not meant as a forum for brands: it was somewhere for individuals to network. However, many organisations started to use it as an effective channel and by 2011 this was recognised, and it is now possible to create a corporate channel on the site.

We suggest taking a similar approach to Flickr as you would to Pinterest. If you have a large number of images that you would love to showcase and encourage people to talk about and share, this may be a viable marketing tool for you.

Setting up an account

To open an account on Flickr, go to www.flickr.com and choose how you would like to log in. There are three options:

1. via a Yahoo! account
2. using Facebook
3. via a Google account (though you will still need to have a Yahoo! account).

If this is to be a corporate account, we suggest you create a Yahoo! account along the lines of mycompany@yahoo.com.

Just as you would with any other social media account, complete your profile, add a profile picture (usually your logo) and carefully choose a keyword-rich or brand-specific URL so that you can easily be found on the site (e.g. www.flickr.com/mycompany).

Unlike sites such as Twitter, Facebook or YouTube, you cannot customise your site. On Flickr, the most important aspect is the images and how you create the folders.

An excellent example of a brand that uses the site is the Ford Motor Company (www.flickr.com/fordmotorcompany). The UK Trade and Investment Department has also used the site as a communications forum (www.flickr.com/ukti).

Creating content

Once you have set up your profile, you will want to start filling it with content, so you'll need to start uploading photos and images. This can be done via your PC or from your mobile device. As you would in Facebook, caption the images and tag people in them. Once you have a number of images, you can sort them into sets (folders). It is then also possible to further categorise sets into collections, making it possible for you to showcase your images to best effect.

We recommend that you do not try to put any content that is too sales-based on the site. Remember that it is not a sales channel. Depending on your business objectives – brand recognition, humanising your brand – you want to post images that will interest visitors to the site and get them to engage with your site by leaving comments and sharing.

Ensure that you tag all your images with appropriate keywords to ensure that they can easily be found by the Flickr social search engine.

Sharing on Flickr

Remember that Flickr is a social network, so it is a good idea to 'Favorite' or 'Add to Gallery' other people's or brands' content on the site as well as leaving comments, where appropriate. As on LinkedIn and Facebook, there are also millions of groups that you can join. This could be used as a networking opportunity or as a way to connect with like-minded organisations or individuals.

The more you engage as a brand, the more content you post and the more creative you are with your images, the more visible you will be on the site.

Finally, as with many other sites, it is possible to share images from Flickr via Twitter and Facebook.

Ways to use Flickr for business

- Creative industries can showcase ideas and images to help give some depth to their brands.
- Highlight events and tie them in with Twitter to give an online account of activity.
- Showcase some testimonials.
- Create Sets for members of staff to humanise your brand.

Tumblr

Tumblr, which was set up in 2007, is a social network based around blogs – a cross between Twitter and WordPress.

According to ComScore, 50% of Tumblr's visitor base are under the age of 25. Teenagers aged 12–17 are about twice as likely as the average internet user to visit Tumblr, while 18–24-year-olds are nearly two and a half times as likely. So, while many youngsters may be turning away from mainstream sites like Facebook, they are clearly embracing alternatives such as this site.

Tumblr could be an excellent way to find a wider audience for your blogs as well as create an engaged community of people who are interested in your thoughts. *Time* magazine is successfully using the site (http://timemagazine.tumblr.com) to share some of their articles. In fact, many newspapers and magazines use Tumblr to build their audience and find a wider reach for their brands: see http://gq.tumblr.com, http://life.tumblr.com and http://rollingstone.tumblr.com.

The site acts very much like a news feed with a combination of articles, images and videos which can then be Liked or reposted in much the same way as content on Facebook. And, as you can do with sponsored stories on Facebook, you can now pay for highlighted posts on Tumblr – which currently costs a few dollars.

Setting up an account

As with all social media accounts, it is important to have a corporate email address with which to sign into Tumblr. Visit www.tumblr.com and hit Sign Up to create an account. Fill in your email, make up a brand-specific or keyword-enabled username, then come up with a suitable password. After being asked if you want to find contacts you know via Facebook and Gmail, you will be asked to verify your email address.

Once your account is set up, you need to configure it correctly. Hit the Settings tab and you will be able to add an avatar, choose a theme for your page, customise how you want people to see or find you on Tumblr and decide whether you wish to send your posts directly to Facebook or Twitter.

Posting on Tumblr

At the top of your page you will see this menu:

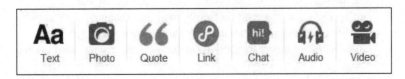

Depending on the type of content you wish to publish, you can choose from each of seven options. When clicking the Aa text tab, you will be taken through to a window which looks much like WordPress.

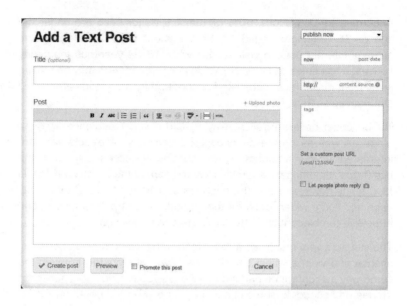

Similar to WordPress and other blogging dashboards, you can format the text and add images, video, audio and links. The usual rules apply.

- Start with an engaging and keyword-friendly headline.
- Use short, snappy paragraphs.
- Break up text with line breaks and images.
- Use inbound links.
- Make sure the text is keyword-enabled.
- Keep it short – no more than 400 words.
- Sign off with a signature containing your applicable contact details.
- Think about using guest bloggers.

Tumblr has recently brought in the option to promote your post so that it will reach a wider audience. You can either pin the post for $5 or highlight the post for $2.

There are also other ways of adding content to the site.

- Posting photos is very similar to Facebook – you upload an image, then caption it.
- It is also possible to upload videos from YouTube or Vimeo.
- Audio posts are powered by Spotify and Soundcheck.
- Quotes and links work in much the same way as in blogs.
- Chat Posts are a way to encourage conversations with other users.

Treat your Tumblr account as you would your website or Facebook Page. The more engaging, regularly updated content you can post, the better.

Sharing on Tumblr

Building your audience on Tumblr involves sharing information and seeking out people and brands that are of relevance to your organisation. On Twitter, one of the best ways of building your community is to start following people who post interesting tweets. Then start following their followers. The same is true of Tumblr.

Finding Blogs enables you to find interesting posts, while using the Explore function (www.tumblr.com/explore) enables you to select from a range of different categories as well as Tags, similar to hashtags on Twitter.

When you find content that you like, you can do three things:

1. comment or post on it
2. favourite it
3. share it (similar to retweet on Twitter).

Because Tumblr is a social network, the more engagement you have with others in the community, the higher the profile of your brand or organisation will be.

Ways to use Tumblr for business

- It could be a great way to engage with younger audiences who are bored with Facebook.
- It's a useful forum to find a wider audience for your blogs.
- As a research tool to find new trends and organisations.
- Thought leadership.
- Feedback mechanism for new products.

MySpace

Once *the* social network, MySpace has seen a lot of changes over the past nine years. From its glory years in 2005–2008, the website saw a real decline which corresponded with the rise in Facebook. Now with 25 million users, the site was relaunched in September 2012 with a ground-up redesign which aimed to make it competitive once more.

One of the key USPs of MySpace has always been its focus on music and that continues to this day. Unsigned musicians can use the site to post and sell music, enabling them to start building a fan base. This is how the artist Lily Allen came to the public's attention. If you are a musician or want to engage with a community of musicians and artists, MySpace may well be a forum for you. However, we believe it is not likely to be a viable option for most other organisations – unless you want to use it to raise your personal profile at corporate level.

MySpace is an interesting example of how companies can go in and out of fashion rapidly. Many people now refer to Facebook in the same way as they did MySpace six or seven years ago – *the* place to be. There are two lessons to be learned here.

1. Don't put all your eggs into one basket. You need to have visibility for your organisation across a number of sites.
2. Keep an eye out for what your audience/potential customer base is doing. If you are getting diminishing returns from one social network, you may find that users are migrating to other social networks instead.

Setting up an account

Go to www.myspace.com and create your account, using either your own name or the name of the band that you represent. There is an option to select whether you are using MySpace personally or as a musician. You then need to fill in some basic information as well as supplying a profile image. You will also be asked to select your own personal MySpace URL. Clearly, if you are using this as an organisation, you would make this applicable to your brand, e.g. www.myspace.com/mybrand.

Then add the people/artists you are interested in, search for any of your friends who are on the site and complete your own profile. You can also customise your profile. Check out this video from Dailymotion for more details: http://dai.ly/V4Xypu.

Posting and sharing on MySpace

In common with other social networking sites, you can post a variety of content, including music, links, photos or videos. If you have a personal MySpace account, you will not be able to upload your own music – you will need to have a Musician account. However, you can share music as well as uploading your own photos and videos to your page.

It is very simple to share content. You can Like, Comment or Share, as you would on Facebook or Tumblr. Remember, the more content you create and the more you share/network on the site, the higher your profile will be.

Ways to use MySpace for business

- If you are a musician or band and want to reach an engaged audience.
- If you want to raise your profile with music lovers.
- Research.

Foursquare

Introduced in 2009, Foursquare is essentially a location-based service for use on mobile devices. Users of the site 'check in' at locations – based on GPS data – to earn points and build their communities. The site is similar to the Check In button on the mobile version of Facebook. On Facebook, users can check in to different locations to alert the people in their network about where they are and what they are doing. Foursquare takes this to a whole different level – the act of checking in forms the basis of the site. It also rewards customer loyalty.

On Foursquare, users can:

- check in to different locations
- get recommendations for places to visit
- explore different venues/locations/places of interest in their area
- earn 'badges' by checking in to locations, often using a given 'tag'
- become a 'mayor' by being the person who checks in the most at a specific location
- load content onto venue/location pages such as recommendations, comments, links or photos.

Setting up a Foursquare business account

1. Set up a personal Foursquare account.
2. Find your venue or listing on Foursquare by searching in the site.
3. Claim this venue as yours. You will see on the right-hand side of the page a tab that says, 'Do you manage this venue? Claim here'.
4. Verify that you are the manager of the establishment. This is done via phone or email.

Once this is done you can use Foursquare as you would a Facebook Page, with updates and content relevant to your target audience. Always remember that the more engaging the content, the better.

You might also want to reward your best customers with a range of sweeteners – money-off deals, freebies and loyalty schemes. Having a business presence will also enable you to have what Foursquare refers to as a Merchant Dashboard. Very similar to Google Analytics or Facebook Insights, it enables the business owner to see how effective their campaigns have been.

> **Note**
>
> For an excellent case study of how a brand has used Foursquare, check out their own page: https://foursquare.com/business/merchants/casestudies/radioshack.

Ways to use Foursquare for business

- Any customer-facing business with a physical location could use the site to increase brand awareness, reward customer loyalty and build an engaged group of fans.
- Think about creative campaigns using deals to encourage people to check in to your venue or location.
- Grow your brand locally as well as further afield by having an interesting and engaged presence on Foursquare.
- Work together with other locations to build networks of complementary businesses.

Social media marketing action plan

- Look at the array of social networking sites on offer and see whether they are likely to meet your organisation's business objectives.
- Work out a strategy for using each of the sites.
- Test and measure to see if the different channels are working for you.
- Regularly ask or poll your target audience to ascertain which social networking sites they are using.
- Never assume anything. Just because some social networks may be viable for your organisation now, they may not be in the future. Remember what happened to MySpace.
- Contact organisations in your network to find out how they have fared with specific sites, what has worked for them and what hasn't.
- A final word. You **must** have free Wi-Fi at your location. Without it, your fans or users may not be able to get online and check in. The cost is negligible and can be recouped very quickly.

11| Pulling it all together

> **What you will learn from this chapter:**
>
> - Understanding how to grow your business
> - Putting together business and marketing strategies
> - Creating a social media 'culture' in your organisation
> - Making sure your website is up to the job
> - Understanding the importance of a content pipeline
> - Finding out about community management
> - Keeping up to date with developments in marketing

Throughout this book, we've kept up the mantra Plan, Listen and Analyse **before** you Engage.

- Plan your objectives.
- Do your research.
- Understand what it all means and what you need to get in place.

Before you . . .

- Dive in and Engage.

Be prepared!

As we've highlighted throughout this book, often the planning seems a bit back to front. Because the social channels are relatively simple (and usually free) to set up and get started on, many people rush to get on board with social media, without really thinking the whole game plan through.

Social media activity isn't about doing it for its own sake. It's fundamentally about delivering on your business objectives. It's taking a step back and thinking about the bigger picture.

From a business objectives perspective, an organisation's objectives will be highly specific. However, fundamentally, most businesses are keen to continue to grow. And therefore, there are just four basic principles that sit at the core of most business growth strategies.

1. **Keep customers coming back for more.** Increasing the frequency of purchases; getting customers to keep coming back to you. This could relate to the customer experience, or the fact that the product or service you sell offers a reason for them to keep coming back to you.
2. **Increase average spend – get the customer to buy more.** A great example of this is the classic McDonalds training mantra, *'Would you like fries with that?'* Consistently getting your customers to buy more from you when they do buy. Amazon do this so well with their 'people who bought this also bought . . .', then bundling offers.
3. **Increase the number of customers.** Getting new customers, then – of course – retaining them, increasing frequency of purchase and increasing average spend.
4. **Increase the effectiveness of each process in the business.** Creating effective systems and processes to create significant business efficiencies.

When you look at business objectives with a top-line focus, rather than broken down into specifics, you can see that social media activity lends itself very well to delivering on these key growth objectives.

Let's take each point in turn and see how social networking activity ties in with it.

1 Keep customers coming back for more

Via social media you can have continuous one-to-one and one-to-many conversations. The fact that customers can engage, share ideas, discuss issues directly with the brand or organisation builds a relationship. You can develop a direct dialogue with your audiences – growing loyalty and rapport, giving them a good reason to keep coming back to you.

2 Increase average spend. Get customers to buy more from you

We've already talked about the 'recommendation generation'. People trust what others have to say more than they trust brands and advertising. When customers are on your website and are researching or looking to make buying decisions, if they see social signals from their friends or other people highly recommending or praising a complementary product or service, they are more likely to trust their views than your promotional messages. If they've made a purchase from you and they see rave reviews for a complementary product or service, they may be more inclined to add that product or service to their basket too.

3 Increase the number of customers

The net can be thrown very wide across social networks. The opportunity for fans to spread the message to other fans is vast. The virality of the platforms means that information and offers can be shared at the touch of a button. Whether campaigns are driven by incentive or by the sheer delight of a service engagement, the reach potential is significant.

4 Increase the effectiveness of each process in the business

As we have shown in this book, social media cannot be viewed in isolation from the rest of your marketing strategy. There are also few parts of your organisation that may not be touched in some way by social media – customer relations, sales, marketing, internal communications, HR, recruitment and even the way your business is structured and resourced. We have stressed the importance of having a proper strategy. Any organisation has goals and must look at the various routes to achieve those goals. Without these it is impossible to grow as a business.

One of the key impacts of social media is that all organisations now need to have a proper, defined marketing strategy. Making assumptions about your target audiences and carrying on doing the same types of marketing is foolhardy and could result in disappointment or even business failure.

What we have demonstrated over the preceding chapters is the breadth and sheer creativity of marketing tools required to communicate in the twenty-first century. Any business now needs to use a number of marketing methods – traditional, web-based and social – to achieve its business goals.

We would advise that you adopt a complementary model, where these are used in combination with each other.

Creating a defined marketing strategy

Going right back to our Plan, Listen, Analyse, Engage model, instead of just focusing on the social media element you need to look at your entire marketing spectrum.

Clearly, your website will be at the heart of your online marketing strategy. It is your most visible online presence (that you own) and is the glue that binds together all your marketing activities. So you need to decide how all the other tools will work in conjunction with it.

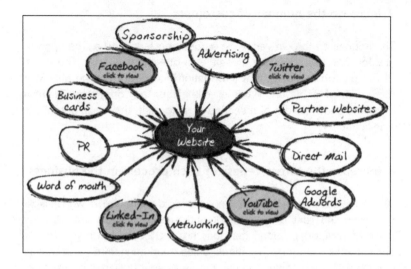

Putting together your strategy

In order to do this properly, there are a number of questions you need to answer as an organisation. We recommend that the management team or senior directors take time out to make sure they focus clearly on these questions. Some of them are fundamental marketing objectives, but we have added a number of new ones that reflect the changing media environment.

- **What are your objectives?** What are you trying to achieve with your marketing?
- **What are your tactics?** What marketing tools will you use to achieve these objectives?
- **What are your key messages?** They should be simple and succinct.
- **Who are the target audience?** Think carefully about the demographic.
- **Where will you find them?** Don't make assumptions about how they consume social media.
- **Where do you send people?** To a website, landing page, social media site?
- **What's your unique selling point?** You may not have one, but try to focus on one or two.
- **What are your keywords?** These are critical to online visibility.
- **How do you get your audience to share?** An integral part of social media campaigns.
- **How do you incentivise your audience?** Give them a reason to like your product or service.
- **How are you going to participate?** It is all about continuous conversations.

- **What are your competitors doing?** Can you do any better?
- **Are you resourced effectively?** Who will assist with marketing? In house or consultancy?
- **What's your compelling content?** Remember, content is king!
- **Does it fit with what your audience want?** Test and measure to see if this is the case.

Once you have looked at all this in detail, you can then start to look at the various channels and marketing tools available to you before putting together your strategy.

Make sure your website is up to the job

We recommend that you take a hard and objective look at your website. Technology is progressing incredibly quickly, and with the advent of mobile internet, your audience may well be accessing your site from a wide range of smartphones or tablets. So is your website really up to the job? Here's a simple 11-point plan for what your website must be and do.

1. **Easy to read, interesting and pertinent to your target market(s):** This may involve having specific landing pages to focus on these target markets.
2. **Reflect the character and personalities of your company and staff:** People buy from people and very often your only real unique selling point will be those who work for you.
3. **Search engine friendly:** Websites have two audiences: humans and search 'bots'. It is important that your site can be found by the search engines so the humans can read it.
4. **On or close to the first page of search engines for key search terms:** 40% of UK websites get no traffic because they don't have a proper SEO and keyword strategy.
5. **Easy to update/have a simple content management system:** You should have control over your website and be able to update it without having to pay costly management fees.
6. **Have a regularly updated and visible news page and/or video feed:** Google is always looking for fresh, keyword-rich content. A news feed or video feed will provide this and reward you with a better position on search engines as well as a heightened awareness of your brand.
7. **Cross-browser and cross-device friendly:** Your site should be built primarily to be seen on mobile devices as well as PCs. It should also look good, no matter what browser you use, whether it's Explorer, Chrome, Firefox or Safari.
8. **Have Google Analytics embedded into all pages of your site:** This simple and free tool from Google will tell you how your website

is performing as well as indicating what effect social media and other marketing activities are having on your web traffic. Do remember to check the analytics regularly and try to set some key performance indicators to track performance.

9. **Include a strong call to action:** As with any other form of marketing, you should encourage visitors to your site to do something – call, email, visit Facebook or sign up to a newsletter. Ideally this should be in the top right-hand corner of your site.

10. **Fast loading:** With so much choice around, people expect immediate results online. Ensure that you don't lose out on valuable visibility because your site isn't fast enough for searches.

11. **Something you are really proud of:** This is your key shop window. If you're not proud of it, what message are you conveying to your target audiences?

Get your website right, and all your other marketing activities will work better. Get it wrong, and all the time you spend on social media may be in vain. After all, if you are driving people back to a website that doesn't deliver, rather than your activity failing, it's the fundamental call to action that isn't working.

Establish a content strategy

In Chapter 3 we spoke about having a specific content creation strategy. Now that you have an overall marketing strategy and a willingness to engage on social media, it is important to work on the content pipeline.

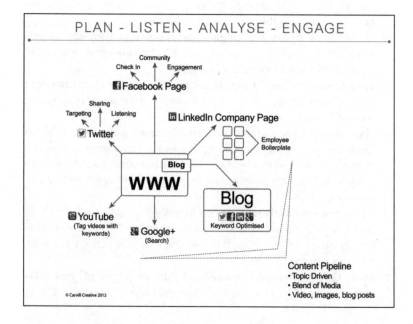

Depending on the number of social media accounts, websites or blogs you manage, there may be a large demand for good, keyword-rich, engaging content and your job is to ensure that there is a steady supply. It's no good having great intentions and setting up a blog or social media accounts only to run out of steam after a few weeks and give up. Remember, social media is all about **continuous** conversations.

You will need regular access to information from within your organisation, high-quality images, videos, ideas for news stories, testimonials and well-written blogs. Where is this going to come from and how are you going to ensure the supply is constant?

Create a social media culture

Once you have a strategy, have earmarked the social media channels that you will be using to meet your specific business objectives and have identified a viable pipeline for content, it is important that you create the correct culture within your organisation as well as setting down your policies and procedures for engaging on social media. You need to establish:

- terms and conditions for your website and social channels
- HR policy for staff using the internet and social media sites
- guidelines for those adding content to your website, blogs and social media sites
- disclaimers.

IBM's Social Computing Guidelines (www.ibm.com/blogs/zz/en/guidelines.html) are seen as a touchstone for how an organisation should embrace social media. Kodak also has an excellent document (www.kodak.com/US/images/en/corp/aboutKodak/onlineToday/Social_Media_9_8.pdf) outlining its terms of engagement with social media.

We have meshed together our own core principles, which you could adapt to suit your organisation's needs.

1. **What you say is permanent and always accessible. You cannot delete an ill-judged status update or post.** It is virtually impossible to remove something from the internet, so exercise caution when expressing an opinion. Any internet post is visible to a huge mix of colleagues, clients, suppliers, competitors, journalists, etc. and even the most obscure topics will be found, so ensure your social activity stays within the Social Media Guidelines.
2. **Be honest about who you are. Don't pretend to be anybody else.** You must always be honest about who you are – but avoid revealing any personal information. If you are talking about [Company Name], identify yourself as a [Company Name]

employee in the content of your post or comment. This is the ethical thing to do, and there may be personal liability under UK law if you don't.

3. **In personal accounts, where relevant, all employees must make it clear that the opinions expressed are their own (and not those of the firm).** Readers *must* know that the opinions expressed are yours rather than [Company Name]'s. You must include a disclaimer notice on every social media profile, e.g. 'Opinions expressed here are my own and do not represent the opinions of [Company Name].' Don't use [Company Name] logos or trademarks unless you have approval to do so.

4. **Be respectful in all communications. Consider how you would like to be treated.** Remember, you have no authority to speak on behalf of [Company Name] (unless this has been explicitly granted), so do not portray yourself as a [Company Name] spokesperson. Despite these caveats, you will be perceived to be the voice of [Company Name], so your actions and behaviours must be appropriate at all times.

5. **Only share information that is in the public domain – never share confidential or sensitive information. Take a common sense approach!** It's clear that certain subjects should not be discussed on social media. If you would not discuss an issue with your friends, why do this openly on the internet? Certain issues should be kept confidential: avoid speculating on future products or services, do not disclose sensitive practice or personal information, and stay within topics that are in the public domain. Be aware of intellectual property issues and avoid discussing financial matters.

6. **Do not engage in discussions with clients or partners around specific work-in-progress issues.** Where relevant, when you do make a reference, link back to the source. Don't publish anything that might allow inferences to be drawn that could embarrass or damage a client.

7. **Mind your manners and treat everybody with respect.** Treat everybody as you would wish to be treated yourself. Never post materials that could be offensive, abusive, threatening or inappropriate. If a discussion escalates into a path you don't wish to go down, simply withdraw from the conversation. Respect the fact that others may have different opinions. Don't get into an argument or battle of opinions online. Don't pick fights, and be sure to be the first to correct your own mistakes.

Protect others and never share their personal information, comments or opinions (unless you have their permission). Be careful when introducing someone to an online conversation as this could affect your relationship and may even create legal or confidentiality concerns. Respect your audience. Don't use ethnic slurs, personal insults, obscenity, or engage in any conduct that would not be acceptable in

[Company Name]'s workplace. You should also show proper consideration for others' privacy and for topics that may be considered objectionable or inflammatory – such as politics and religion.

8. **Understand when an official response may be necessary.** Some topics or issues may require a formal response from [Company Name]. In that case, quickly raise the issue with your line manager or relevant team member so that it can be effectively dealt with before it gets out of hand. If you have any doubts, speak in the first instance with [Named Contact, Tel. _____].

9. **Critical considerations.** Inappropriate comments (e.g. derogatory, offensive, bullying or discriminatory comments towards employees, ex-employees, staff of clients, [Company Name] managers or team, or any comment that potentially or actually brings the firm into disrepute), whether placed on social media sites during working hours or outside working hours, is a disciplinary offence. Furthermore, depending on the circumstances, a single incident can result in dismissal on grounds of gross misconduct for a first offence. Further details of the disciplinary procedures can be found in the Employee Handbook.

   Any breach of these guidelines could be considered a disciplinary issue by [Company Name]. See [Company Name] Handbook for details.

Specific guidelines for social media platforms

Twitter

Twitter corporate: If you are working on one of [Company Name]'s corporate Twitter accounts, you will be acting as the community manager of that account. Therefore, you will be the 'voice' of that account for [Company Name]. This is not a personal account, nor will the person tasked with managing that specific account be named.

Twitter personal: If you have a personal Twitter account and use Twitter for personal use, unless it is agreed that the Twitter personal account will be used as part of [Company Name's] social media strategy the company asks that you ensure a disclaimer notice is added to your account to indemnify any relationship between [Company Name] and that personal account, e.g. 'This is the personal Twitter account of _____. Opinions expressed here are my own.'

Facebook

Facebook corporate: If you are working as the community manager on [Company Name's] corporate Facebook Page, you will be acting as the community manager of that account. Therefore, you will be the 'voice' of that account for [Company Name]. This is not a personal account, nor will the person tasked with managing that specific account be named.

Facebook personal: If you have a personal Facebook account and use Facebook for personal use, the company asks that you ensure that a distinct line is drawn between 'work and play' – for example, the company does not encourage members of staff 'befriending' clients on Facebook. For example, 'My Facebook account is personal and so I do not accept clients or associates from my place of work as friends.'

LinkedIn

LinkedIn Profile: [Company Name] advocates that all employees have an up-to-date and a 100% complete LinkedIn Profile. Where the employee inserts details of being employed by [Company Name] we ask that any references to [Company Name] are made as follows:

Account Manager [Company Name]

Get talking!

As explained earlier in the chapter, social media touch many parts of organisations. We recommend that when putting together a marketing strategy for the business, time should also be devoted to creating a co-ordinated approach to communications, internally and externally.

In larger organisations, the management team or heads of departments should have regular meetings or huddles to discuss any issues that may have an impact on the business and end up in the social domain. Supply problems, staffing disputes, quality control, customer service and supplier complaints could all end up going public. The sooner you have policies in place to deal with these issues, the better placed you will be to prevent them harming your reputation or your brand.

Alternatively, in a smaller organisation you could have a simple weekly huddle to discuss what's happening in customer services, sales, marketing and product development.

Extract information to share

These meetings could also be useful forums to garner information that could be used as content on your social media sites. You may even consider getting together a group of people in the organisation who can act as your social media committee. Their job would be to ensure a steady supply of information and to ward off potential issues before they arise.

This committee's job could also be to instil in all staff the importance of the business being an open organisation and the value that social media could bring. In effect they would be social media champions.

Responsibility for social media

Whatever the size of your organisation, there needs to be a strict delineation of who is responsible for being your representative on social media. Whether you are a one-man-band or a multinational company, you need to have lines of reporting.

Remember that whoever has responsibility is essentially representing the company online, in the same way that a press office or PR agency would represent them to the traditional media. So they need to be well informed, articulate, able to cope under pressure, creative, good listeners, able to synthesise data and information quickly, and be entirely trustworthy. Fundamentally, they've got to know your business or brand.

If you were thinking about getting an intern or a school leaver to be your 'community manager', think again – as you can see, this is quite a skilled and responsible job. You wouldn't let someone who is a trainee mechanic service your Porsche, so don't hand over such a focused form of marketing to someone who isn't trained.

In fact, depending on your business objectives and how you wish to use social media, you may well require more than one person. Companies such as Best Western hotels employ entire teams of community managers to handle different social media accounts.

You may decide to keep all your community management in house, or you may decide to outsource it to an external agency. Each approach has its merits, but one thing to bear in mind is that social media is quite personal and, unlike PR, you cannot delegate it entirely to other people to manage. You still need to be proactive, engaged and interested in what is happening, and feed news that can be used to create relevant content. Even if you've got experts managing the implementation as an extension of your team or brand, it's important that you play a part – and this can be quite time consuming.

Social media community management is a large employment growth area. The role of these staff is solely to manage your social media accounts and devote the necessary time to them in order to deliver on your strategic objectives.

You may consider hiring someone to perform this function, in which case you need to think about the qualities involved. It is vital that your organisation is open to being proactive on social media or, no matter who you have to manage your accounts, they will not have the necessary buy-in to be able to do their job properly. This also applies to any organisation that has outsourced their marketing or PR to an outside agency. Ask yourself: 'Do they have the necessary skills to manage your social media accounts – are they a true extension of my team?'

A typical day of social media activity

Here's a very quick guide to how to go about effective daily social management for general awareness. This schedule is by no means prescriptive and you can work the timings around your organisation's specific requirements.

Clearly, your activity will focus on the objective of specific social media accounts. For example, if your Twitter account is for customer support you'd refine it in line with customer support requirements. Similarly, if Facebook is being used to generate sales leads, mould it to these needs.

This schedule relates to a 'general' awareness, daily PR focus. For each account:

8.30 a.m. – 9.00 a.m. (Or possibly earlier, if you can do this via your mobile device during your commute to work.) Review account activity: check for mentions, direct messages and what your followers are talking about – respond, thank, retweet, engage and react accordingly. How long this takes will depend on your level of 'engagement' and on how many accounts you have. So you may have to revise your timescales here a little.

9.00 a.m. – 10.00 a.m. Scout all relevant trade press, review your Google Alerts, keyword tracking in HootSuite, Twitter search and relevant blogs and portals that you subscribe to, and review any up-to-date and relevant news. Speak to the marketing/sales team or, if relevant, the senior management team and ensure you're up to date on any marketing activities, business news and promotions that can also be shared on your account(s).

9.00 a.m. – 11.00 a.m. At the same time as researching, schedule your day's content into HootSuite (or other social dashboard), blog or Facebook Page. Don't schedule all these updates to follow one another so that you block up your audiences' feeds: spread them out, usually at hourly intervals – and if it's big news, don't be afraid to repeat the message on Twitter, but be sure to give it a different 'spin'.

11.00 a.m. – 11.15 a.m. Check accounts and alerts to review any activity, mentions, retweets, etc., and any engagement.

11.15 a.m. – 1 p.m. Content creation. This activity and the timescale related to it will vary according to how many blogs you're writing and what content (if any) you are creating. You may have determined to create at least one blog post a day – if so, this is your time to create.

Throughout the afternoon . . . Keep watching those alerts, mentions and engagement.

The busiest time is changing . . .

The times when people are most active on social media are changing. At one time, most activity happened in the afternoon and engagement levels were generally higher. With the emergence of smartphones and social apps activity is shifting. Early morning (commuter time), between 6.30 a.m. and 8.30 a.m., is now a busy period for social activity. Lunchtimes are also busy; then there is another spike at the end of the day – 6.00 p.m. to around 7.30 p.m. So be mindful of this when scheduling your updates and looking at engagement. Most Facebook posts get engagement between 11.00 a.m. and 4.00 p.m. and after working hours. So test, measure and learn what's working on the timing front for your organisation.

Finally, remember that each account is an important communication channel and you are acting as 'brand custodian'. It's not just about pushing messages out but more about sharing the personality of the brand as well as engaging and communicating with your audiences.

Staying ahead of the curve with your marketing

The world is changing, technology is constantly evolving and the world's consumption of the media is in a constant state of flux. It is vital that you stay vigilant and keep on top of these changes so that you can make sure that your company is equipped to adapt.

Marketing methods come and go, and so will social media sites. While Facebook may have over one billion users now, it may fall out of favour and a new network take its place, much as happened to MySpace in the mid-2000s.

One of the cornerstones of marketing is the need to test and measure. Keep reviewing your sales figures, the analytics from your website and the return from your social media channels. See if you can spot any emerging trends or areas in which you need to improve.

Once you have a marketing strategy, keep updating and adapting it to the changing times. You may need to overhaul it completely every year, depending on what is happening to your customer base.

At the time of writing, it is impossible to predict what may happen in the coming years. We may see a time when the main channels start charging subscriptions, or we could end up seeing the social networks moving into the marketing verticals or becoming more geographically based (e.g. Twitter.co.uk, Facebook.fr).

There will also always be entrepreneurs and innovators coming up with new ways of communicating, so expect more social networks, more mobile-based applications and better ways of tracking customer movements. With the advent of 4G technology as well as near field communication (NFC), brands and organisations have never had so many ways of engaging with a potentially global audience.

The trick is to harness the technology and understand how to use it correctly. Many companies will also have to change dramatically their approach to communications. Becoming a social business is no easy feat and it may involve a high amount of resistance. However, this is a social age and cheetahs will outrun the sloths.

The other thing to keep in mind is that whilst these channels have been around for a number of years now, we're not yet into decades. From a business strategy perspective, these channels are relatively new and learned best practices and models are fertile territory.

Effectively, we're all learning together.

To end

Developments in social media are moving at such a rapid rate that by the time this book is published, some of it will, alas, already be out of date!

However, fear not – we will keep you constantly updated via the blog we've created to run alongside this book (www.businessofbeingsocial. co.uk) and via Twitter (@BOBSthebook).

Join us on the journey and we hope you'll gain as much from social media as we have. As we said earlier – let's learn together.

Social media marketing action plan

- Institute a full review into your business to establish your strategic goals.
- Create a fully integrated marketing strategy to achieve these goals.
- Make sure your website is up to the job and mobile friendly.
- Work towards creating a social media culture in your organisation.
- Ensure you have a decent content pipeline.
- Test and measure.
- Stay informed and never assume that things will stay the same – business agility is key.

Social media glossary

Twitter

@username: The name you choose to represent yourself on Twitter, this is shown at the beginning of all your tweets and starts with the @ sign.

Direct message: A private message to somebody who is following you on Twitter. A direct message can only be sent to somebody who is following you. You can do this by putting d (not DM) in front of their Twitter name, e.g. d @michellecarvill. Using social dashboards such as HootSuite enables you to send a direct message as one of the standard message features.

Follower: Someone on Twitter who is interested in watching/listening and 'following' what you tweet. They 'follow' your tweets from their account and automatically see your Twitter updates.

Following: When you follow someone else on Twitter. You automatically see their Twitter updates.

Handle: The @username is also sometimes referred to as your Twitter 'handle' (an old CB radio term).

Hashtag (#): The # can be used to categorise your tweet to a particular topic. Then someone searching for the topic will see your tweet. For example, if I were to tweet about this glossary I could hashtag the tweet #twittertips. (For more on hashtags, see www.carvillcreative.co.uk/blog/demystifying-the-hashtag-and-how-to-leverage-on-twitter.)

Klout: Your Klout score demonstrates how your influence is measured on Twitter. It starts at zero and the more people who tweet you, share your tweets on and retweet you etc., the higher your score becomes. Klout is deemed by some as an unfair measure of reach and engagement on Twitter as it measures only basic sharing – fluctuations in Klout scores are often not focused on too heavily.

Locking your profile: You can lock your Twitter profile so that only people you allow to follow you will see your Twitter updates.

Mentions: This is how you can tell if somebody has directly tweeted you, by writing @your username in front of their tweet. You can pick up their message under your 'Mentions'. (Mentions are recorded in a number of Twitter management platforms.)

Microblog: Tweeting is sometimes referred to as microblogging – you are effectively writing a 140-character mini-blog.

Retweet (RT): A retweet is used to repeat a specific tweet. It can be used to reiterate what somebody else has said in agreement or to show all your followers a tweet that you are replying to.

Social dashboard: A dashboard where you bring in all your Twitter feeds into one central place so that you can manage multiple accounts more effectively. Common dashboards include www.hootsuite.com, www.tweetdeck.com and www.cotweet.com.

Tactical retweets: Retweeting the tweet of somebody you want to notice you and follow you back or retweet your tweets

Targeted followers: Targeting the people who listen to your tweets for a purpose and following people you want to follow you back.

Tiny URL: This is the name of one website that shortens your URL so that you don't take up too many of your 140 characters with a link (http://tinyurl.com). There are others, including bit.ly.com. Twitter management platforms such as Tweetdeck, HootSuite and CoTweet either have their own URL-shortening programs or use the more common ones.

Trends: Popular subjects that are being tweeted about; categorised by the hashtag (#). For example, this glossary would appear in the trend #twittertips because that's the subject we have categorised (hashtagged) it to in our tweet.

Tweet: A message (maximum length 140 characters) sent via Twitter.

Tweeter: Somebody who uses Twitter.

Twitter chat: When a group of users on Twitter connect and converse not by following one another, but by following a # around a conversation, e.g. #blogchat or #usguys. These are ongoing conversations, often held at a specific date and time each week or month.

Twitter lists: You can sort your followers into segments by creating lists so that you can better organise your Twitter thread. See here for how to create and manage Twitter lists: www.carvillcreative.co.uk/blog/twitter-lists---what-they-are-and-how-to-use-them-effectively.

Facebook

Business timeline/business page: A business timeline is not a profile. This is a way to promote a business or brand (not an individual)

on Facebook through your personal profile. You cannot become friends with a business timeline, you can only Like it.

Cover photo: A large photo (850 × 315 pixels) that stretches across the top of your timeline, like a banner, just above your profile picture. Cover photos will remain public, even if all the rest of your photos are private. Be aware that there are some strict guidelines on the cover photo for your business timeline (see www.facebook.com/page-guidelines.php).

EdgeRank: An algorithm developed by Facebook to govern what is displayed (and how high) on the news feed.

Facebook personal timeline: Your timeline represents you personally and not as a business. It is your own personal profile, in which people can see a 'timeline' of your activity, photos and wall posts since you joined Facebook. It is a way to share information about yourself with others in order to socialise and network.

Friends lists/smart lists/close friends: A way of organising your 'friends' into lists giving you options as to who sees what.

Friends: Other people on Facebook who want to link themselves to your profile and follow your activity.

Group: Usually created by brands, companies, organisations and individuals to drum up support or to promote something. You can Like a group and/or become a member of that group.

Insights: Analytics that show how a user's Facebook Page is performing. Shows interaction, users and reach.

Like: If you Like something on Facebook it means that you approve of whatever is being represented, promoted, shown or discussed. You can Like videos, statuses, business pages, people, photos, groups and discussions.

Network: A group of people who have joined together on Facebook who have something in common, usually a business, school or university network.

Notifications: Facebook notifies you with optional messages that let you know if any activity has occurred on your Facebook.

Poke: If you poke somebody on Facebook you are interacting with them, you are virtually 'poking' them. It's as simple as that.

Profile picture: A small picture (200 pixels wide) that appears on your personal or business timeline. It will appear on the site to represent you whenever you comment, post or Like anything on Facebook. Your profile picture on a business timeline is most likely to be your logo or company branding, whereas on your personal timeline it will probably be a picture of you.

Status update: This is described by Facebook as the way you can 'give positive feedback and connect with the things you care about'. Status updates contain information that you want to share with people connected to your Timeline – personal or business-related. The status may contain a picture, link or video.

Stream: This is where all activity is logged instantaneously from your friends' personal profiles, business pages and groups you have liked. It is a way of keeping up to date with everything that is going on in Facebook.

Tagging: Being mentioned in a status update or identified in a picture. You are notified when you have been tagged.

Wall: This appears in your Facebook timeline. It's a space that allows other people on Facebook to post messages to you that everybody can see.

LinkedIn

1st-degree connections: Direct connections with people who you know on a personal level.

2nd-degree connections: Connections to your 1st-degree connections.

3rd-degree connections: Connections to your 2nd-degree connections.

Company profile: A company profile is connected to the employees/people related to it. Company profiles can be populated with products and service information.

Connections: Similar to friends on Facebook, 'connections' is the term used when you link yourself to other people you wish to be associated with on LinkedIn.

Groups: Groups on LinkedIn allow professionals to advance their careers by sharing expertise, experience and knowledge on a specific subject. You can search groups and join relevant groups or create your own groups.

Introduction: Messages that allow members to contact you or be contacted through a shared or mutual connection.

Invitation: An invitation sent to an existing member of LinkedIn to join a network.

Networks: A group of LinkedIn users who can contact you. They can be up to three connections away.

Profile: Your personal profile, in which you can showcase your expertise, skills and recommendations. It's your personal brand.

Recommendations: This is when somebody is recommended on LinkedIn. Users usually ask business partners, colleagues or service providers or clients to 'recommend them'. They are effectively online referrals/testimonials.